Rhetoric and Praxis

Rhetoric and Praxis

The Contribution of Classical Rhetoric to Practical Reasoning

edited by Jean Dietz Moss

The Catholic University of America Press
Washington, D.C.

PE
1404
R 49
1986

Printed in the United States of America
24.⁰⁰

Library of Congress Cataloging-in-Publication Data
Main entry under title:
Rhetoric and praxis.

Papers presented at a conference held October 6-8,
1983 at the Catholic University of America in
Washington, D.C., sponsored by the National Endowment
for the Humanities and Catholic University of America.
Bibliography: p.
Includes index.
1. English language—Rhetoric—Study and teaching—
Congresses. 2. Rhetoric, Ancient—Congresses.
3. Reasoning—Congresses. I. Moss, Jean Dietz.
II. National Endowment for the Humanities.
III. Catholic University of America.
PE1404.R49 1986 808'.042'07 85-25449
ISBN 0-8132-0619-7

46598

Contents

Preface

The purpose of this book of essays like the conference that gave them life is to develop an area of classical rhetoric, rarely treated at length, that could be used to advantage by teachers in the present day. The area focused on might be called practical reasoning or, more specifically, logical investigation and rational judgment. That many students do not develop their thoughts clearly and logically on paper is a complaint voiced by teachers from many disciplines. But this flaw is not restricted to the college classroom. It abounds in public speeches and in reporting and writing of all kinds, which may explain the popularity of the current expression "Where's the beef?" Exasperation at a speaker's or writer's difficulty in getting to the heart of the matter and setting it forth cogently is voiced almost universally.

In a conference jointly sponsored by the National Endowment for the Humanities and The Catholic University of America, six well-known scholars in the fields of classical rhetoric, philosophy, and college composition presented the results of their own studies of classical rhetorical techniques for approaching this problem, describing for the participants those methods that might be adapted to modern composition classes. The conference, entitled Classical Rhetoric and the Teaching of Freshman Composition, was held on the campus of The Catholic University of America in Washington, D.C., October 6–8, 1983, and was attended by more than one hundred college and university professors from around the nation. They set to work immediately to rough out teaching materials based on the suggestions outlined in the papers. These ideas were revised and circulated among the participants for field testing; then they were revised again and readied for general distribution. Thus, the emphasis of the conference was not simply on how these particular methods had worked in the past but rather on how they might be used today.

This volume contains the papers presented at the conference, published here in hope that they will continue to serve as a catalyst for teachers, or, for that matter, for anyone who is curious about the efficacy of classical methods of practical reasoning for writing and speaking.

Our special thanks must go first to the National Endowment for the Humanities and to Blanche Premo, who coordinated the grant for NEH, and to the president of The Catholic University of America, the Reverend William J. Byron, S.J. Next we owe the success of the conference to its lecturers: Richard J. Schoeck, University of Colorado–Boulder; Edward P. J. Corbett, The Ohio State University; Maxine C. Hairston, University of Texas–Austin; James L. Kinneavy, University of Texas–Austin; William A. Wallace, The Catholic University of America; and George R. Bramer, Lansing Community College. The conference participants were given considerable aid by the discussion leaders: Richard E. Young, Carnegie-Mellon University; John Poulakos, Pennsylvania State University–Delaware Campus; Lois M. McMillan, Morgan State University; Barbara Stout, Montgomery College; and Rosemary Gates, The Catholic University of America.

Finally, we must express our deep gratitude for the assistance of the two conference coordinators: Kathleen Millar Imbemba and Brother Daniel Adams. Brother Adams was responsible for the smooth running of the conference activities, and he also typed the teaching materials and book manuscript; Mrs. Millar Imbemba developed the teaching materials with unusual sensitivity and ingenuity.

JEAN DIETZ MOSS

Notes on Contributors

GEORGE R. BRAMER is chairperson of the Department of Communication at Lansing Community College, Lansing, Michigan. Formerly he was coordinator of Writing Programs in English at West Virginia University and director of Freshman English at Creighton University. He is coauthor of *Process One: A College Writing Program* (Columbus, Ohio: Charles Merrill, 1977) and *Writing for Readers* (Columbus, Ohio: Charles Merrill, 1981). A member of the National Council of English Committee on Public Doublespeak, he has contributed articles to *College Composition and Communication, College English, The English Journal,* and other publications. Dr. Bramer has directed federally funded institutes for secondary teachers of composition and media and served as a consultant in teacher preparation programs.

EDWARD P. J. CORBETT is Professor of English at The Ohio State University and the former Director of Freshman English at that school. He is currently the Chair of the College Section of the National Council of Teachers of English, and the Executive Secretary of the Rhetoric Society of America. The author of *Classical Rhetoric for the Modern Student* (Oxford University Press, 2nd ed., 1971), he also wrote the introduction to the new Modern Library College Edition of *The Rhetoric and the Poetics of Aristotle* (Random House, 1984). *Essays on Classical Rhetoric and Modern Discourse,* ed. Robert J. Connors, Lisa S. Ede, and Andrea A. Lunsford (Southern Illinois University Press, 1984), is a festschrift published in his honor.

MAXINE C. HAIRSTON is Professor of English and Rhetoric at the University of Texas–Austin, where she teaches rhetorical theory, the pedagogy of writing, and writing courses at all levels. She is the author of *A Contemporary Rhetoric* (Houghton Mifflin, 3rd ed., 1982) and *Successful Writing* (W. W. Norton and Co., 1981); she has also written "Not All Errors Are Created Equal," published in *College English* (December 1981), and three articles that appeared in *College Composition and Communication:* "Working with Advanced Writers" (May 1984), "The Winds of Change: Thomas Kuhn and the Revolution in the Teaching of Writing" (February 1982), and "Carl Rogers' Alternative to Traditional Rhetoric" (May 1980).

JAMES L. KINNEAVY, Professor of English and Rhetoric at the University of Texas–Austin, is also Director of the Graduate Rhetoric Program. He is the author of a number of articles on rhetorical theory and pedagogy. His influential book, *A Theory of Discourse* (Prentice-Hall, 1971), has been reissued (W. W. Norton, 1980). Dr. Kinneavy has also coauthored three composition textbooks. In addition to his writing and teaching, he has served as a consultant for composition programs in more than twenty-five colleges and universities. His theoretical framework was adopted as the basis for the language arts program in grades one through twelve for the State of Texas.

JEAN DIETZ MOSS is Associate Professor of English at The Catholic University of America, where she directs the Rhetoric and Composition Program. She teaches courses in the history of rhetoric, pedagogy of composition, and rhetorical theory. She is also a Renaissance historian, the author of a number of articles on the rhetoric of science and religion, and of a book on a religious sect of the Reformation period, *Godded with God: Hendrik Niclaes and the Family of Love* (American Philosophical Society, 1981). Her articles have appeared in the *Renaissance Quarterly, The Sixteenth Century Journal, The Journal of English Teaching Techniques,* and *College Composition and Communication.*

RICHARD J. SCHOECK, Professor of English and Humanities at the University of Colorado, has taught at Cornell, Notre Dame, Toronto, Princeton, and the University of Maryland. He has also served as chairman of departments of English (St. Michael's College, Toronto), Integrated Studies (Colorado), and Comparative Literature (Colorado), as well as Director of Research

Activities of the Folger Shakespeare Library. He has published articles on medieval and Renaissance rhetoric, and his most recent publication is *Intertextuality and Renaissance Texts* (Bamberg, 1984).

WILLIAM A. WALLACE is Professor of Philosophy and History at The Catholic University of America, where he regularly teaches courses on Aristotle's *Posterior Analytics, Physics,* and *Rhetoric.* A past president of the American Catholic Philosophical Association, he is currently Director General of the Leonine Commission, an international group of scholars preparing critical Latin editions of all the writings of St. Thomas Aquinas. He is the author of ten books, including the two-volume *Causality and Scientific Explanation* (University of Michigan Press, 1972-1974), and some 250 articles in scholarly journals and encyclopedias. Apart from his interest in causality, on which he has published extensively, he has recently been examining the sources of modern science in medieval and Renaissance thought as recorded in Galileo's early Latin notebooks.

Jean Dietz Moss

I Prolegomenon: The Revival of Practical Reasoning

The essays in this volume were composed with one common aim: to retrieve from the classical age of rhetoric some methods of practical reasoning—methods of stimulating and ordering thought about matters of common concern—that might inform our teaching of writing today. The authors focus on five important concepts of classical rhetoric: the *topoi,* the enthymeme, *kairos, aitia,* and *telos.* The first two terms figure prominently in the most influential treatise on the subject, Aristotle's *Rhetoric.* The other three are not developed in detail there, but they do underlie much of its content, and other philosophers and rhetoricians of the classical period emphasize them when considering rhetorical practice.

At the base of these studies is the belief that the act of reasoning has not changed since the time of the Sophists, Plato, and Aristotle, although the art of reasoning has assumed various forms. But the nature of the human mind, its powers of apprehending and of reasoning, is the same today as it was yesterday. This belief does run counter to some current opinions holding that "revolutions in epistemology" have replaced the thought processes of the past.[1] Classical rhetoric, we are told, was founded upon the sand: it taught that we could make "reasoned judgments about experience."[2] But scepticism about whether we can know anything is a philosophical stance that has had its advocates since the time of the pre-Socratics. Gorgias voiced such a view when he said that knowledge was impossible to attain and impossible to convey.[3] The implications of this philosophy for rhetors was that any method of persuasion that worked was acceptable. This approach made the term rhetoric an epithet. The sophistic rhetor's aim to meet any occasion and audience and emerge victorious generated prescriptive handbooks and an emphasis on virtuosity that has been part of the history of rhetoric down to our time.

Another approach to rhetoric—the Platonic-Aristotelian one—assumes that knowledge is attainable, that reason is a process native to the mind and that rhetoric can consciously avail itself of this dynamic to discover what it shares or does not share with an audience, and that it can present this persuasively. In this view, the dynamic process that yields knowledge is essentially a moral enterprise, whose aim is to discover what is and what appears to be true for the benefit of both the searcher and the audience. It assumes that audiences believe that knowledge is possible and

1. This is the opinion of C. H. Knoblauch and Lil Brannon in *Rhetorical Traditions and the Teaching of Writing* (Upper Montclair, N.J.: Boynton/Cook, 1984), p. 23. The authors take a militant anti-classical view of rhetoric because of the great changes they see in our methods of uncovering knowledge (see chap. 2). Their understanding of epistemology and the processes of invention in classical rhetoric is not shared by all scholars.

2. Ibid. An evaluation of rhetoric and epistemology different from Knoblauch and Brannon is in John Gage, "An Adequate Epistemology for Composition: Classical and Modern Perspectives," in *Essays on Classical and Modern Discourse,* ed. Robert J. Connors et al. (Carbondale, Ill.: Southern Illinois University Press, 1984), pp. 152–169.

3. A translation of Gorgias's "On Being" is in Kathleen Freeman, *Ancilla to the Pre-Socratic Philosophers* (Cambridge, Mass.: Harvard University Press, 1957), pp. 127–128. For an illuminating discussion of the Sophists, see Larry Arnhart, *Aristotle on Political Reasoning: A Commentary on the Rhetoric* (De Kalb, Ill.: Northern Illinois University Press, 1981), pp. 3–53. See also George Kennedy, *Classical Rhetoric and its Christian and Secular Tradition* (Chapel Hill, N.C.: The University of North Carolina Press, 1980), pp. 25–40.

that they would like to act on what has been established as true or probably true. Our judicial processes are founded on this belief, and laws are created with the understanding that they will be obeyed, not equivocally but truthfully. Juries attempt to ascertain what probably happened in the past in arriving at a judgment. For the Platonic-Aristotelian tradition, the kind of reasoning involved in making decisions about the proper action to take in the future is also a kind of probable reasoning. It assumes that, although the contingencies of nature and of individuals prevent our obtaining certainty about future political and social affairs, we still can use our reason to discover the best course to pursue.[4] Such reasoning applied to human affairs to make decisions about what should be done is rhetorical reasoning issuing in *praxis,* and it was the central concern of the participants in this conference.

Classical rhetoric has been described as a prescriptive or formulary art that trammeled the creativity of the students trained in it and does the same thing to modern students who are taught it.[5] That description contains elements of truth, but it does not perceive that classical rhetoric denotes not just one approach; rather it is a generic term for what was taught by the Sophists, Aristotle, Cicero, and Quintilian, among others, in the classical period. The prescriptive character of rhetoric was in evidence before Aristotle wrote his *Rhetoric,* and some adaptations of his strategies of invention produced a repertoire of stock responses that were far different from the dynamic process he had conceived them to be. Professor Corbett discusses these conceptions of *topoi* in his essay in this volume. Other adaptations of Aristotle, however, produced the *status* questionary, so useful in focusing judicial issues, described by Professors Schoeck and Bramer in their

---

4. This point is, of course, the basis for Chaim Perelman's writings on rhetoric and justice. See *The New Rhetoric* (Notre Dame, Ind.: The University of Notre Dame Press, 1969), which Perelman authored with L. Olbrechts-Tyteca, and his *The Idea of Justice and the Problem of Argument* (London: Routledge and Kegan Paul, 1963).

5. Knoblauch and Brannon are representative of many who conceive of classical rhetorical training as essentially prescriptive. See pp. 25–31.

essays. Thus this negative evaluation of classical rhetoric is based upon a rhetoric shorn of the reasoning dynamic contained in the *topoi,* and expressed artfully in enthymeme and example, the conceptions of appropriateness and timeliness of *kairos,* and the necessity of framing discourse in regard to its end or *telos.*

The reason that a revival of some of these forgotten or neglected elements of practical reasoning seemed an appropriate aim for our conference should become more apparent if we pause at this point and briefly consider some critical junctures in the fortunes of this elusive component of rhetoric. Professor Schoeck, whose essay follows, will treat its nature and historical development in more detail.

The art of rhetorical reasoning transmitted by the Roman rhetoricians, as we have already suggested, had lost some of the nuances of Aristotelian rhetoric. The three modes of proof: *ethos, pathos,* and *logos* and their interactions, the concept of probable reasoning and its relationship to issues and audience apparently were not fully understood. The prescriptive character of the art began to predominate after the classical period as occasions for *praxis* diminished in the West with the breakdown of the political, judicial, and social systems in which it had once flourished. The two major texts through which rhetoric was taught in Europe during the Middle Ages, Cicero's *De inventione* and the pseudo-Ciceronian *Ad Herennium,* furnished students with techniques of reasoning that had limited practical value at the time. They were put to use mainly in the school exercises of declamation. Formulary rhetoric was the refuge of many of those who were engaged in the public communication of chanceries, courts, or commercial enterprises in the Middle Ages.[6] Although distinctly a rhetorical art, Christian preaching did not avail itself of the techniques of practical reasoning sketched out in the classical tradition, either. As George Kennedy has pointed out, "Christian preaching is . . . not

6. Kennedy discusses these aspects of medieval rhetoric and the fate of what he terms "philosophical rhetoric" in chaps. 4 and 9. See also James J. Murphy, *Rhetoric in the Middle Ages* (Berkeley: University of California Press, 1974), pt. 2.

persuasion, but proclamation based on authority and grace not proof."[7]

Thus rhetorical reasoning, formerly so important for political, ceremonial, and judicial discourse, lay almost dormant during the early Middle Ages, but it was picked up and remolded in the techniques of argumentation for the popular disputations of the universities of the twelfth and thirteenth centuries. The reasoning part of rhetoric was absorbed by dialectic.[8] Eventually the energy and creativity with which positions were argued died away as the disputation became an empty university requirement, an occasion for the display of stock positions. Interest in dialectic in many universities withered with it.

When classical rhetorical texts were rediscovered in the Renaissance, the study of rhetoric was revitalized. The writings of the ancients were read in the original Greek and Latin and were appreciated first of all for their beauty of expression and then for their relevance to contemporary life. Humanist scholars sought the Ciceronian ideal: eloquence wedded to wisdom. Thus the *studia humanitatis* came to embrace not only grammar and rhetoric, but also poetry, history, and moral philosophy. A course treating such works as Aristotle's *Rhetoric* might examine them from several angles: the philological and literary, the moral, the political and historical.[9]

Although the citizen-orator was a classical model that inspired early Italian Humanists, their fascination with classical oratory

7. Kennedy, p. 127.

8. Richard McKeon brilliantly surveys the relation of rhetoric to logic in "Rhetoric in the Middle Ages, *Speculum* 17 (January 1942): 1–32. See also the important study by Wilbur Samuel Howell, *Logic and Rhetoric in England, 1500–1700* (Princeton, N.J.: Princeton University Press, 1956).

9. The subject matter treated in the courses does not follow strict disciplinary lines. My own research on the records of the Universities of Pisa and Padua in the sixteenth century shows that rhetoricians or grammarians might lecture under any number of designations: "Greek" or "Greek and Latin" or "Ethics and Greek," and by the end of the century "Humane Literature." There they might treat in the same course works related to moral philosophy, rhetoric, poetry, or drama. For example, at the University of Pisa under the title, Greek and Latin, Domenico Mancini Cortensis read the *Rhetoric* of Aristotle and followed it with Sophocles's *Antigone*, Archivio di Stato, Pisa, Ms. G. 77, fols. 170–233.

was mostly engendered by the eloquence of the rhetor. That eloquence might be brought to serve practical aims and moral improvement, but the method of achieving similar results was most often that of imitation and not of systematic instruction in the art of rhetorical reasoning.[10]

During the late Renaissance, in some colleges and universities, a return to rhetorical reasoning was combined with the study of the classical texts. For example, the Collegio Romano, the Jesuit college in Rome, carried the teaching of rhetorical reasoning to a level it had not attained since the days of the Lyceum. During the later half of the sixteenth century, the Jesuit professors brought to the rhetorical art of invention new *topoi* derived from dialectic, and these wedded to the tradition of dialectical reasoning infused new life into the study of practical reasoning. Since the *Ratio Studiorum,* the program of studies at the Collegio, was adopted by Jesuit colleges and universities throughout Europe and imitated by some secular universities, the influence of this scholastic revival of rhetoric was broader than has been realized.

The renewed interest in Aristotelian rhetoric and *praxis* at the Collegio was not destined to dominate the subsequent history of rhetorical education. While the full Ciceronian tradition—which included the five parts of rhetoric: invention, arrangement, style, memory and delivery—continued to be taught in many schools throughout Europe and Great Britain, other approaches became popular as well. In northern Europe the reforms of Peter Ramus

10. For a treatment of the relationship of rhetoric to civic affairs, see Eugenio Garin, *Philosophy and Civic Life in the Renaissance* (Oxford: Basil Blackwell, 1965); and Jerrold Seigel, *Rhetoric and Philosophy in Renaissance Humanism* (Princeton, N.J.: Princeton University Press, 1968), especially chap. 8. See also Brian Vicker's essay on the relevance of epideictic rhetoric to civic life, "On the Practicalities of Renaissance Rhetoric," in *Rhetoric Revalued,* Medieval and Renaissance Texts and Studies, vol. 19 (Binghamton, N.Y.: Center for Medieval and Early Renaissance Studies, 1982), pp. 133–142. The most influential studies of philosophy, rhetoric, and humanism are those of Paul Oskar Kristeller. On the subject of rhetoric and logic, see "The Scholar and his Public in the Late Middle Ages and the Renaissance," in *Medieval Aspects of Renaissance Learning,* ed. and trans. Edward P. Mahoney (Durham, N.C.: Duke University Press, 1974); and "Philosophy and Rhetoric from Antiquity to the Renaissance," in *Renaissance Thought and its Sources,* ed. Michael Mooney (New York: Columbia University Press, 1979).

separated the process of invention from rhetoric and assigned it to logic, and this accentuated the tendency to focus on style in the teaching of rhetoric already strong in the *studia humanitatis*.[11] The fragmentation of rhetorical teaching was fostered also by an anti-Aristotelianism that had existed side by side with the revival of Peripatetic rhetoric. The distaste for Aristotle provided the climate for the development of rationalism, which eschewed any attachment to scholastic logic. For Descartes and the Port-Royalists, truth is attained in a self-evident judgment such as that found in an axiom of geometry. Reasoning should begin at that point, they believed, and from there attempt to arrive at obvious conclusions. The indisputable truths of science are the goals worth seeking, and logic should govern the quest and monitor the scientist's thinking to keep it on course. Probable reasoning on contingent affairs, they thought, cannot discover truth and is therefore a useless process. Furthermore, the use of emotion to move audiences is really just an attempt to manipulate them.[12] Interestingly enough, Galileo, considered to be the father of modern science, used a wide range of rhetorical strategies with unabashed zeal, including emotional appeals, to persuade his audience to accept Copernicanism.[13]

Sir Francis Bacon and some scholars who followed him returned to the dynamics of probable reasoning as a necessary part of the study of rhetoric. Bacon believed, however, that true inven-

11. See Walter Ong, *Ramus, Method and the Decay of Dialogue* (Cambridge: Harvard University Press, 1958). Karl Wallace remarks on the effects of Ramus's reforms in "The Fundamentals of Rhetoric," in *The Prospect of Rhetoric*, ed. L. F. Bitzer and E. Black (Englewood Cliffs, N.J.: Prentice-Hall, Inc., 1971), pp. 10–11.

12. Kennedy, pp. 215–222, discusses the effect of the Cartesians, and Chaim Perelman takes great pains to point out the need for his new rhetoric in the wake of the havoc wrought by the new philosophy, *The New Rhetoric*, pp. 1–4, which he reiterates in *The Realm of Rhetoric* (Notre Dame, Ind.: University of Notre Dame Press, 1982), p. 7. Karl Wallace surveys the Bacon-Ramus-Descartes revolution in "The Fundamentals of Rhetoric," pp. 10–11.

13. I discuss some of Galileo's uses of rhetoric in "Galileo's *Letter to Christina*: Some Rhetorical Considerations," *Renaissance Quarterly* 36 (Winter 1983): 547–576; and in "Galileo's Rhetorical Strategies in Defense of Copernicanism," in *Novita Celesti, Crisi del Sapere*, ed. Paolo Galluzzi (Florence: G. Barbèra Editore, 1984), 95–103.

tion belonged only to the scientist and method to the logician, further adding to the fragmentation of the components of rhetoric. The net effect of the rationalism of Descartes and the empiricism of the members of the Royal Society was to make of "scientific method" a new golden rule by which all other reasoning was to be measured.

The effects of the influence of the Ramists, the rationalists, and the empiricists on the art of rhetoric were countered to some degree in eighteenth-century Europe by the stature accorded it by Vico. He understood the nature of rhetoric in the classical sense, the importance of invention and probable reasoning, and he saw the necessity of adapting discourse to the character of the audience. Neoclassicism in Great Britain took a different direction. Influenced by empiricism, and especially the new associationist psychology, George Campbell held that thought grew out of associations of experiences within the mind or reflections upon these experiences. This new epistemology led him to discount the efficacy of practical reasoning and to concentrate instead upon psychology.[14] By the end of the eighteenth century, practical reasoning was severed from rhetoric and appeared only briefly in the rhetoric and logic of Richard Whately and in the lectures of the first two Boylston professors at Harvard in the early nineteenth century. Not until the mid-twentieth century was there a real revival of interest in the full panoply of classical rhetoric.[15]

During the 1960s, enthusiasm mounted for a reexamination of the full rhetorical tradition of classical times for what it could offer to the teaching of English composition. The pioneering effort was Edward P. J. Corbett's *Classical Rhetoric for the Modern Student,* first published in 1965. Professor Corbett demonstrated the efficacy of classical techniques of invention and rhetorical reasoning for students in the modern age. Then in 1970, the Wingspread Con-

---

14. See Kennedy, chap. 11; and K. Wallace, "The Fundamentals of Rhetoric," p. 11.

15. See the discussion of nineteenth- and twentieth-century developments in Edward P. J. Corbett, *Classical Rhetoric for the Modern Student* (Oxford: Oxford University Press, 1971), pp. 625–630.

ference brought together scholars from departments of speech, English, and philosophy in order to establish a new footing for classical rhetoric in all of these disciplines. As a part of the Rhetoric Project sponsored by the National Endowment for the Humanities, the participants in the Wingspread Conference and the deliberative session that followed looked at the role of rhetoric in the past and speculated about its future.[16]

Two of the final recommendations of the Rhetoric Project might be regarded as the mandate for the essays in this volume, for they furnished the inspiration for the aims of the Conference on Classical Rhetoric and the Teaching of Freshman Composition at Catholic University, where the papers were first presented in 1983. One of the recommendations addressed the necessity for rational deliberation and communication in our time: "A clarified and expanded concept of reason and rational decision must be worked out." The nature of rhetoric's special contribution to this concept was further articulated: "It is precisely this area of the contingent, the relatively uncertain in which rhetoric has had its primary application. . . . Rationality applicable to procedures of investigation and judgment must be devised and widely taught, so that rational decision marks our choices in the area of the contingent."[17]

The other recommendation is closely related to the first. It points to the importance of invention in preparing the way for rational decisions, saying that "rhetorical invention should be restored to a position of centrality in theory and practice." The concepts and strategies for analyzing problems, discovering and defining issues, developing lines of argument or proofs, and assessing and evaluating propositions are all a part of invention. The authors add that "this branch of rhetoric has been largely neglected since the eighteenth century when theorists influenced by revolutions in science and philosophy dismissed *inventio* as

16. The papers, responses, and reports of the deliberations are included in *The Prospect of Rhetoric.*
17. Ibid., pp. 238–239.

trivial on the assumption that a single methodology—namely the new science—should be used by sensible people in all kinds of investigations and deliberations."[18]

The influence of these recommendations and the Wingspread papers are still being felt. The seventies saw a great revival of interest in rhetoric, especially in invention. Some extensive studies and a number of teaching approaches in composition have been concerned with reviving the old heuristics and inventing new ones. The annual bibliography of rhetorical studies in the *Rhetoric Society Quarterly* bears witness to the growth of scholarship in this area. A special supplement devoted to heuristics alone was published in 1982, including almost eight hundred entries, the bulk of these having appeared since 1970. Today a preponderance of textbooks contain sections on invention, contrary to the practice in early 1974 when I reviewed the coverage of that topic for *College Composition and Communication* in two pages.[19]

The other topic referred to in the two recommendations we have mentioned above from the Wingspread Conference, practical reasoning, has not had such an enthusiastic revival. Unfortunately, the battles of philosophers over certainty and probability have occupied the varied parties of analysts and intuitionists, leaving barren ground for most writers in the composition field. Only a few artifacts remain that the teacher dares describe for the edification of freshmen. The scanty and timid treatment of induction, deduction, the enthymeme, and the fallacies in most textbooks has more the appearance of ritualistic observance than any belief in their applicability to problems or situations.

Only a few of the most popular college writing texts for freshmen devote more than two to five pages to thinking or reasoning using classical methods, exclusive of the discussions of fallacies.[20] These few actually illustrate induction and deduction, show-

18. Ibid., p. 239.

19. Review article, *College Composition and Communication* 25 (February 1974): 56–57.

20. Those texts that devote greater length to reasoning are Maxine Hairston, *A Contemporary Rhetoric* (Boston: Houghton Mifflin, 1982); Frank D'Angelo,

ing their relevance to analyzing the thought of others and to developing topics, but even then the enthymeme is gingerly discussed, if at all. Some recent texts do introduce adaptations of Stephen Toulmin's approach to logic; however, these attempts to provide a clearer and simpler method are even more complex than the older ones. Moreover, many instructors are as bewildered by the new approach as by the old. Earlier texts—such as Corbett's *Classical Rhetoric* (1965) and Young, Becker, and Pike's *Rhetoric: Discovery and Change* (1970)—integrated classical practical logic into the teaching of composition naturally, and with copious illustrations, but these valuable texts were considered too difficult for ordinary freshmen. Thus the most essential skill for developing and ordering thought for communication is rarely taught to college freshmen in a manner relevant to its use. Training in rhetorical reasoning may be available in some colleges and universities in practical logic courses, but these are not required of most students and for a majority they are not available.

The objective of the conference and of the papers in this volume was not simply to reexamine induction and deduction, but to take from the study of these areas what is pertinent, adding to them other classical methods of analysis—the *topoi,* the enthymeme, principles of causal explanation, and the evaluation of ends or intentions of discourse. This last aspect of practical reasoning is a topic that occupied classical rhetoricians at length, but it is ignored by contemporary teachers of writing even though it is a subject that troubles students and professional writers alike.

It is encouraging to find support for the focus of the conference in recent research on learning theory as it relates to the teaching of writing. Carl H. Klaus says that in the University of Iowa's Institute on Writing, sponsored in part by the National Endowment for the Humanities, the basic assumptions guiding the new courses developed there in the five-year program are the following: that students at the freshman level are ready to move into

---

Process and Thought in Composition (Cambridge, Mass.: Winthrop, 1981); and W. Ross Winterowd, *The Contemporary Writer* (New York: Harcourt Brace Jovanovich, 1981).

persuasive and referential discourse, and that learning should take place by problem-solving techniques rather than through modeling or following a set of rules.[21] The Iowa courses are based on the theories of Dewey, Bruner, Piaget, and Vygotsky.

Following in the direction of these studies, the papers presented here attempt to provide instruments for students to apply to problems and issues in the college classroom and in the world outside. In the next essay, "The Practical Tradition of Classical Rhetoric," Richard J. Schoeck traces the emphasis of rhetoric on practical affairs throughout the course of its history. His was the keynote address of the conference, and appropriately so, for he first drew my attention to the need for a conference to address the topic of *rhetorica praxis*. His own research on the teaching and practice of rhetoric at Oxford in the fourteenth century and on the use made of rhetoric by lawyers in sixteenth-century England, from which inferences can be drawn about education in rhetoric at the Inns of Court, demonstrate his interest in the subject.[22]

One of the major observations Professor Schoeck makes in his essay is that Ciceronian rhetoric served not only as a static exemplar to be imitated in later ages, but also as a model to be adapted to the practical concerns of religious and secular life. The pragmatic use of eloquence to preserve civic morality was Cicero's and Quintilian's enduring concern. The methodology for developing persuasive discourse outlined in their works was practiced in schoolroom exercises for the ultimate purpose of moving an audience to action, not just to induce admiration for the author's or orator's brilliance. The ideal of wisdom and eloquence at the service of society was carried forward, Schoeck shows, by John Henry Newman in his *Idea of a University*. Today the need for

21. Carl H. Klaus, "Research on Writing Courses: A Cautionary Essay," *Freshman English News* 11 (Spring 1982): 1–13.

22. "On Rhetoric in Fourteenth-Century Oxford," *Mediaeval Studies* (1968): 214–225; "Rhetoric and Law in Sixteenth-Century England," *Studies in Philology* (1953): 11–115; and "Lawyers and Rhetoric in Sixteenth Century England," in *Renaissance Eloquence: Studies in the Theory and Practice of Renaissance Rhetoric*, ed. James J. Murphy (Berkeley: University of California Press, 1983), pp. 274–291.

such a conception of rhetoric is even greater, as specialization in science further compartmentalizes knowledge and reduces communication of its subject matter to quantificational vehicles— charts, graphs, and statistical tables. But the mathematical model is not sufficient to analyze and express the goals of political, social, and private affairs. For these purposes we need rhetorical methods, and we may as well return to those that have proved their efficacy over the centuries.

Edward P. J. Corbett begins the reexamination of techniques of the past in his essay entitled "The *Topoi* Revisited." He has treated the *topoi* extensively in his seminal treatise, *Classical Rhetoric,* where they still serve as a resource for teachers interested in classical methods. Here he is concerned with showing how these ancient *topoi* were used in the past and how modern authors have devised new *topoi* to complement the old.

Professor Corbett first examines the *topoi* or topics as devised by Aristotle, pointing out their complex nature, some parts of which have been largely forgotten. Topics were not only finding devices for a particular subject matter, as the "special" topics were; they were also intended to be patterns or forms of inference, the "common" topics—common because they can be used to explore any subject. Since the common topics are believed to mirror the way in which the mind reasons naturally, they are appropriate devices to probe subjects—not just exercises for their amplification, as they became in the hands of later Roman and Renaissance teachers.

Richard Young, as Corbett notes, has been instrumental in drawing attention to heuristic devices in another of the original senses, that of a dynamic process yielding unpredictable results. The tagmemic system Young advances is a new set of *topoi* that might be used along with those of Aristotle. Kenneth Burke's pentad has also been appropriated by composition teachers as yet another set of modern *topoi*. Finally, when canvassing other prospects for *topoi,* Corbett suggests that they might even be employed to program computers so that vast stores of information could be unlocked at will. On reflection, one might say that this would be a use of special topics far beyond anything that the compilers of Renaissance commonplace books could envision. But there would still be a need for the unprogrammed inferential reasoning of the common topics to discern relationships, to assess degrees of difference, and to evaluate material as related to a particular audience and occasion.

Corbett surveys the fecundity of the topic system and provides many examples of its continued relevance to the teaching of writing. But lest there still be objections to its classroom use by those who say that nobody really uses the *topoi* in developing discourse, some further observations are in order.[23] First, since the heuristic devices are thought to mirror the way in which the mind works, we might assume that the mind naturally tends to ask the kind of questions the *topoi* propose, and it does so unconsciously. In other words, most of us use the *topoi* unsystematically and without realizing it. Again, formalizing a set of questions in a topical system provides us with a simple means of monitoring our coverage of the possibilities. In this way the topics provide a more focused and broader range of probes than, for example, that furnished by the popular brainstorming techniques of gathering associated ideas—often haphazardly and in a time-consuming manner.

Moreover, Aristotle's *topoi* are part of a much larger theory of reasoning. Looking briefly at the way in which they relate to other modes of reasoning in his philosophy enables us to see the scope of our focus in the conference and to understand its value and limitations. The distinctions Aristotle makes also offer interesting insights into the way reasoning is generally viewed in the modern world. The origin of the *topoi* lies in the *predicables* or the ways in which we speak about things and analyze them. We look at the *genus* or class under which a large number of items might be grouped, and we consider the *differences* that separate these items into subgroups or *species.* We think of a species as having a certain nature that entails various *properties;* we also note that beings in

23. See Arnhart, pp. 13–21.

these species have variable characteristics or *accidents* not essential to their nature. The *topoi* express these basic aspects of things in the world around us and how they are related one to another. For Aristotle, reasoning is concerned with two kinds of matters: those that can yield true and certain knowledge because we can ascertain their causes, the domain of science; and those where so many contingencies exist that we can arrive only at what is probably true, the domain of dialectics and rhetoric. In the logical treatises that make up the *Organon,* Aristotle includes an analysis of probable reasoning that he appropriately titles the *Topics.* Here he develops a handbook for dialectical reasoning; he further calls attention to that work in his *Rhetoric,* noting there that it is useful for persuasive discourse as well.[24] What separates the two arts of dialectic and rhetoric is that rhetoric is aimed at moving an audience, whereas dialectic ignores audience to concentrate on the subject matter through the use of reason alone. Of the three appeals that the rhetorician uses to move an audience—*ethos,* the appeal from the character of the speaker; *pathos,* the appeal to the audience's emotions; and *logos,* the appeal from reason—only the last is common to the two arts.

The complexity of the *topoi* and the enthymeme in their formal and material natures may explain why the subjects have largely been neglected by teachers of composition. But one need not trace these foundations in order to teach them. Fortunately Maxine Hairston's contribution to this volume, "Bringing Aristotle's Enthymeme into the Composition Classroom," describes both the form and the matter of the enthymeme in such a clear and informal manner that teachers will find the subject immediately accessible. After explaining the peculiar nature of this form of practical reasoning as outlined below, she gives many examples of how it

24. *The Rhetoric of Aristotle,* ed. Lane Cooper (New York: Appleton-Century-Crofts, 1932), Book 1, pp. 6, 10, 16; Book 2, pp. 157, 163, 165, 177, 181; and Book 3, p. 239. William M. A. Grimaldi has a fine discussion of the nature of the topics in *Studies in the Philosophy of Aristotle's Rhetoric, Hermes, Zeitschrift fur Klassiche Philologie* 25 (1972), especially pp. 134–135.

might be employed in writing tasks. The result is a unique contribution to understanding and reviving this powerful tool of persuasion.

In his concern for reasoning in rhetoric, as Professor Hairston notes, Aristotle stresses that the enthymeme and the example are the two devices appropriate to it. The materials from which enthymemes and examples are devised are provided through the topics, the philosopher further explains. And he refers his students to the *Topics* for clarification and additional examples. Since the *Rhetorica* and the *Topica*, like all of Aristotle's surviving treatises, are composed of lecture notes collected by others, some particulars seem less than clear, and a vast body of commentatorial and interpretative literature has grown up around them. From the text that remains and from the commentaries, ancient and modern, one can derive certain clear characteristics of the *topoi*. As Corbett also notes in his essay, the *topos* or topic as used by Aristotle has a dual nature. It consists of a dynamic strategy of inquiry and a subject matter to which it is applied. The matter may be specific to a discipline, or it may be common to all.

It is in this way that the *topoi* are closely related to the enthymeme, for the latter depends upon techniques of topical invention to provide the ground from which premises may be drawn. Focusing on this connection enables us to bridge the matter contained in Corbett's and Hairston's essays respectively. In form, the enthymeme resembles the syllogism, having a major premise, a minor premise, and a conclusion, although all of these components are not articulated, as they would be in a dialectical argument, because this might weary the audience. The distinctive feature of the enthymeme is that it depends upon the audience's adherence to, and tacit acknowledgment of, certain beliefs, opinions, and values to generate conviction or proof. These beliefs, opinions, and values are the common ground the rhetor simply assumes; he does not need to articulate them since they are obvious to his audience. They generally furnish the unexpressed premise that, were it expressed, would complete a formal syllogism. For Aristotle, persuasion consists in aiding an audience to reach a decision by presenting matter pertinent to it. That presentation must take into account the natures of the individuals who make up the audience, and these natures are composed of character, emotion, and reason. On this account, persuasion appeals to the whole person.[25] Emotion is not something to be despised as an ignoble part of a person's being, as it came to be viewed with the Port-Royalists and the later intellectuals of the Enlightenment. Rather it is an important spring to action, for it encompasses the values and opinions that are held most dear. The power of the enthymeme resides in the simple fact that it can touch upon such fervently held ideas.

The studies of Hairston and Corbett provide new insights into these two, well-known techniques of classical rhetoric. The three essays that follow introduce three unfamiliar but significant concepts for the teaching of rhetoric and composition today, concepts important in the lives and thought of the classical world that can enlarge and redirect our own consideration of issues and problems. The three—kairos, aitia, and telos—are Greek terms that pertain to the most central concerns of man in society: timeliness, causes, and ends or goals. Each of the scholars who offers his observations here has thought about his topic for years and is deeply convinced of its importance in reasoning and in communication that is authentic and responsible.

In a highly original essay, "Kairos: A Neglected Concept in Classical Rhetoric," James L. Kinneavy calls for a reexamination of kairos, that is, timeliness and fitness, a concept of great importance in Sophistic, Platonic, and Ciceronian rhetoric. It was linked to the ideal of justice by the Pythagoreans and hence has implications that are moral as well as pragmatic. As Kinneavy points out, the concept has been almost ignored by rhetoricians since the ancient period, although it has appeared in the last sixty years in the writings of several Italian scholars interested in classical rhetoric and in the theology of Paul Tillich. Kinneavy observes that kairos, even though not explicitly acknowledged, is implicit in the

25. Arnhart, pp. 9–10, 37–43.

notion of "situational context" used in a number of disciplines and in that of "rhetorical situation" as developed by Lloyd Bitzer for speech communications.

After an enlightening exegesis of the many levels of meaning of the term in times past—ethical, educational, epistemological, and aesthetic—Kinneavy proposes the adoption of *kairos* as the central concept of a composition program. He demonstrates the consequences of such a program in each of the areas previously defined: the ethical choices that would be revealed, the social issues that would have to be examined, the responsibility for rhetorical communication that would be awakened in students beginning their education in any discipline, and finally the aesthetic awareness and sensitivity that would be cultivated in such a program.

William A. Wallace brings to the next study, "*Aitia:* Causal Reasoning in Composition and Rhetoric," a philosopher's expertise in analysis and a particular interest in the contribution of Aristotle to scientific questions and to reasoning in general. Looking at the manner in which a consideration of cause can inform our teaching of rhetoric and writing, he provides a new *topos* for use by modern writers in many disciplines and for all kinds of writing.

In the introductory section of his essay, Father Wallace traces the concept of causality, showing its place in the science of Aristotle and its subsequent history.[26] He then describes vividly its usefulness as a tool of analysis in the realm of general knowledge. Over the centuries the concept lost the richness of Aristotle's analysis and came to be viewed in rhetoric simply as a sequence of cause and effect, appearing in the repertoire or techniques for paragraph development. Handbooks for composition tell us that we might want to focus either on the cause or causes of something or the effects. We hear of necessary and sufficient causes and incidental factors in more sophisticated treatments of the topic, but the fourfold nature of causality itself as it was described in the writings of Aristotle is never mentioned. Ironically, as Wallace

26. Wallace is the author of an extensive study of causality, *Causality and Scientific Explanation,* 2 vols. (Ann Arbor: University of Michigan 1972, 1974).

has shown, what began as a scientific tool of analysis has become more useful to laymen, who must be concerned with causes in everyday affairs, while scientists speak but rarely of the causes of physical phenomena. The topic of causality as it is developed here also greatly interested Renaissance scholars. I have recently discovered notes for lectures given at the Collegio Romano, the Jesuit College in Rome, that treat the subject in great detail, citing Aristotle as the authority for their analyses. Those of the Jesuit Peter Perpinan, preserved in a manuscript dating from 1563, devote ten folios to an explication of the fourfold nature of cause and its various uses in discourse. It seems likely that the great attention given to logic at the college fostered such interest in the role of *aitia* in rhetoric. Other authors of the same period whose works derive from the Jesuit tradition treat the same material at even greater length. One such, who published extensively, plagiarizing Jesuit materials in other subject matter and probably in rhetoric as well, devotes fifty-odd pages to the topic.[27] Fortunately, in his unique and inventive treatment of the concept, Wallace is able to restore an instrument of analysis capable of revealing to us much in the way of complexities and nuances that otherwise might be hidden.

Aitia is closely related to the subject of ends, as Wallace points out, and George R. Bramer addresses this subject in the final essay of the volume, "Right Rhetoric: Classical Roots for Contemporary Aims in Writing." This is another aspect of classical rhetoric that deserves attention today, for it troubles both students and professional writers. Aristotle implies in his *Rhetoric* that the function of that art is to enable man to live a rational life.[28] To do so requires making judgments, but the judgments related to the practice of rhetoric are rarely discussed in composition texts.[29]

27. The materials related to the teaching of rhetoric among the Jesuits in Rome and further afield in Northern Italy are part of a study in preparation.

28. Arnhart discusses rationality and the ethics of Aristotle's rhetoric, pp. 24–30.

29. See the discussion of this point in Gerard A. Hauser, "The Most Significant Passage in Aristotle's Rhetoric or How Function May Make Moral Philosophers of Us All," *Rhetoric Society Quarterly* 12 (Winter 1982): 13–16.

Since Watergate, concern has grown among English teachers about "doublespeak." Many textbooks admonish students to avoid jargon and faceless prose. But what is needed is a systematic treatment of the teleological concerns of rhetoric. For this we must go beyond discussions of tone, persona, and voice, of connotation, logic, and the fallacies to reach the underlying problem of honesty and good will articulated in classical rhetorics.

Young, Becker, and Pike make ethical considerations the theme of their text. Their treatment of Rogerian argument introduces a radical shift in the goal of argument from victory to cooperation. They ask students to look carefully at another person's point of view and present it respectfully. In the wrong hands, however, such a technique might be used to manipulate an audience, indeed much more than the classical style of argument it was designed to replace.[30]

Two recent articles in prominent journals devoted to rhetoric and composition emphasize the need for attention to the ethics of rhetoric and call for careful treatment of the issues in the classroom. Allen Ramsey states that "the ethics of rhetoric are bound up with the success of rhetoric."[31] Students should be taught to analyze purpose and to be clear about why, as well as what, they are writing. As David V. Harrington points out, ethical writing is not just a matter of honesty and consideration for others.[32] He thinks that students must be shown that it takes "insistent inquiry to get to the heart of a problem" and that there is an ethical necessity to check and recheck data. The high ethical standards of academic writing, he suggests, should serve as a vehicle to demonstrate the seriousness with which scholars approach a topic. Thus, for him, *praxis* is inextricably bound up with ethics.

30. Richard E. Young, Alton L. Becker, and Kenneth Pike, *Rhetoric: Discovery and Change* (New York: Harcourt, Brace and World, 1970). John T. Gage suggests that in setting forth Rogerian argument as a series of steps or a formula as some textbooks do, the authors may imply unwittingly that it is a powerful tool for manipulation simply because it pretends not to be, pp. 164–165.

31. "Rhetoric and the Ethics of 'Seeming,' " *Rhetoric Society Quarterly* 11 (Spring 1981): 85–96.

32. "Teaching Ethical Writing," *Freshman English News* 10 (Spring 1981): 13–16.

Professor Bramer, who has been concerned with the problem of aims in discourse for some time, presents in this essay a program for analyzing and distinguishing among ends that illuminates the problems and offers a guide for decision making. He separates the proximate goals of content, or the desired effect on an audience, from the ultimate aims that motivate the consideration of the subject matter in the first place. Ultimate aims he sees as the final values and goals one desires, and he suggests that these are two: truth and harmony. Drawing upon Platonic and Aristotelian conceptions of rhetoric and modern writers' treatment of moral choice, he shows how these twin goals lie at the base of our social, political, and private decisions. Bramer works carefully through the various stages of writing, indicating how these concepts may be applied at each stage, and drawing out the implications of each.

This completes the major contributions of the Conference. In looking back over the six papers one sees that there is really far more here than a recovery of the classical tradition. Each of the authors has added insights of his and her own, thus renewing the original ideas. That is a revival in the full sense of the word, and a further testimony to the enduring inspiration that the wisdom of the ancients can provide for those who are inclined to inquire into it.

Richard J. Schoeck

2 The Practical Tradition of Classical Rhetoric

In the long sweep of rhetoric—a two-millenium long road that takes us from Isocrates' noble reaction against Gorgias and sophistical rhetoric in the late fifth and early fourth centuries B.C.; to other Greek rhetoricians; to Cicero and other Roman orators, lawyers and rhetoricians; to Augustine; to the Middle Ages and the Renaissance; and finally to our own age—throughout this long sweep it seems to me to be quite remarkable how some of the fundamental truths discovered by ancient theorists and then put into practice by the host of practioners of one of the oldest of professions (we cannot and we dare not call it the oldest profession) are now being rediscovered. But mankind seems to want to reinvent the wheel over and over again, as we in academe observe so frequently, and we have all witnessed in this or that literary critic a M. Jourdain transplanted from Molière's *Le Bourgeois Gentilhomme* who discovers that he has been speaking rhetoric all his life.

One of the jargon terms of our generation is *strategy*. We are "besieged" (to pursue the military dimensions of the metaphor) by the language of the Pentagon, and there are strategies of war-games (now threatened by the invasion of computers) as well as of the actual battlefield, and there are the strategies of the administrators who spend more time before their pet computers than before books or in hearing their faculty speak. We have long witnessed real strategems as well as the art of using strategems in politics, business, courtship, and other battlegrounds and arenas, perhaps none more ferociously fought than in the battles of the boardrooms and ratings conferences of Madison Avenue. But how often have we considered the parallels between strategy and *inventio*? And, given the determination of a long-range policy, the deployment of one's forces and the attention to logistics, or, in the house of rhetoric, *dispositio*? One might well continue this paralleling, but only at the risk of moving into a fully developed medieval allegorizing of the game—as they did with chess or with one or another of the liberal arts, as Chancellor Jean Gerson of Paris did with grammar in his *Donatus moralizatus*—all of which saw a correspondence, if not a moral *significatio,* in every move, position, part, or piece of the game.

Rather, my point is a simple one: the art of rhetoric is one of our oldest and most enduring inheritances from the classical period, and it has never lost its usefulness or its relevance to the widest possible spectrum of problems and situations in a long sequence of changing societies. I want to begin, therefore, by providing as a background for the papers that follow a sense of the place and importance of that most fundamental of the parts of rhetoric, invention, during the classical period. Then I will call attention to the absorption by dialectic of this fundamental part of rhetoric during the Middle Ages and, finally, indicate the profound change, almost the revolution, which took place during the Renaissance—the effects of which we are still experiencing in our culture's valuation of rhetoric. If my point is a simple one, that of stressing the enduring usefulness and practicality of rhetoric, my tactic will be that of the *synecdoche:* by developing a clearer picture of the fortunes of invention, I hope to suggest the larger fortunes of rhetoric during its long history and to urge that we reaffirm our belief in classical rhetoric.

From one point of view, then, my purpose is to set the stage for the contributions of Professors Corbett, Hairston, Kinneavy, Wallace, and Bramer, who have come to grips with particular issues of rhetoric and the problem of teaching writing in our society. But from another point of view one of my tasks or responsibilities is to call to mind the continuum. During the long stretch of time from its beginnings twenty-five centuries ago until today, rhetoric has always been thought to be highly practical, and the relation between the theory and practice of rhetoric and the society it serves is one which will tell us much about the value that society puts upon rhetoric, recognizing its need and its potential value—especially in the estimation of the individual's capacity and responsibility for making decisions and responding rationally to eloquence. There is a vast difference that separates both the speech and the estimation of audience in Pico della Mirandola's late fourteenth-century Oration on the Dignity of Man, for example, from a twentieth-century example like Nixon's Checkers speech on the American political scene. The genre of *apologia* might be thought the same, but the values clearly have changed. Pico was a fourteenth-century Florentine humanist who valued the dignity of man; Nixon abused the genre and had little respect for humanistic values.

Rhetoric, I repeat, has always been one of the most practical of studies and professions. For what could be more practical than an art which permitted one to attain mastery in the three comprehensive kinds of eloquence: judicial (*genus iudiciale*); deliberative oratory (*genus deliberativum*); and panegyrical or epideictic oratory (*genus demonstrativum*)? These three embrace the whole field of eloquence and most, if not all, of the spheres of human public activity, and they prepare one to function in situations in which the speaker is called upon or volunteers to move and persuade his fellows. Small wonder that the Renaissance—especially after Bruni and Valla—saw eloquence as the high reach of man in society and the civic humanist who could practice eloquence as the greatest of men. But even more than this attention to the importance of the three kinds of eloquence there is another effect of rhetorical training: a sound rhetorical training cultivated the habit of practical reasoning. Even in the Middle Ages when rhetoric became subordinated to dialectic (one need think only of the thrust and parry of logic in the disputation and quodlibet) there was still a role for rhetoric, and indeed there is a need to inquire more searchingly into the role of rhetoric in scholastic writing, to study rhetoric in St. Thomas Aquinas, for example. In the Middle Ages rhetoric was subordinated, but it was never abandoned.

But when we move into the late fifteenth and early sixteenth centuries and witness the pressure of humanists to elevate the role of rhetoric, and within the university curriculum to substitute new rhetoric for the medieval and to replace the previously dominant logic of the scholastics by humanistic rhetoric, then we can see the multiplicity of ways in which the humanists made use of rhetoric to develop practical reasoning. Perhaps a single illustration will serve. In his controversy with the *nouveau theologien* Martin Dorp, who had attacked Erasmus, Thomas More attempted to construct a quasi-logical, quasi-juristic case in defense of Erasmus and humanism, and then at a crucial point he interrupted himself with a fine rhetorical gesture. A syllogism, he said (having just developed one), was "not a syllogism for the reason that it is properly constructed in accordance with the precepts of dialectics and fashioned as a *barbara* syllogism, but because reason, which made such a rule for that very purpose, tells us that the conclusion follows from the premises."[1] In one sentence an overdependence upon dialectical rules has been swept away, and More cunningly argues that reason is greater than logic.

However, I have been moving too rapidly, and I want to go back to look at the function of invention among the ancients and then to follow that line of development through the Middle Ages and Renaissance.

Nunc quid ago et dubiam trepidus quo dirigo prorant? This line from Paulinus of Perigueux in his life of St. Martin (II, 6) speaks of the difficulty that every writer faces. As Curtius comments in

---

1. *Selected Letters of St. Thomas More,* ed. Elizabeth Frances Rogers (New Haven: Yale University Press, 1961), p. 23.

his use of the line: "The author has to take breath and find new strength";[2] and this line, expressing as it does one of the oldest of *topoi,* the modesty or humility *topos* (which is to be found in the Old Testament in its special form of self-disparagement), may serve both to introduce a new part of my text and at the same time to indicate the resourcefulness of the topics of rhetoric: they are indeed the stock room of the classical system, and we must be indebted to Curtius for showing us their long life as part of the continuity of the classical tradition. As with any stock room, rhetoric stores up the topics to be used and provides a system or philosophy for making use of them; then the value of each new use will be a function in part of the new context and in part of the energy endowed by the latest writer (although Curtius does not usually address this question). And so, in trepidation before the matter at hand, one may with Paulinus ask: *What do I do? Where shall I fearfully steer my uncertain boat?* In response to such a self-reflexive question (as we have learned to call it), I respond that I wish to focus on the tradition of invention, a part of rhetoric on which nearly every writer has touched, but none among recent scholars has treated it exhaustively or definitively. I also want to comment upon rhetoric in the service of contemporary society at each moment of new theory and practice.

There are, as every student of rhetoric knows, five parts of a discourse, which were recognized as early as Aristotle; and the first and in many ways most crucial part is *inventio,* to use the Latin term instead of the Greek *heurisis;* the modern English equivalent is, of course, *invention* or *discovery.*[3]

Under *heurisis* in Greek rhetoric came several possible modes

2. Ernst Robert Curtius, *European Literature and the Latin Middle Ages,* trans. Willard R. Trask, Bollingen Series, no. 36 (Princeton, N.J.: Princeton University Press, 1967), p. 79.
3. According to the *Oxford English Dictionary, invention* was first used by Stephen Hawes in his *Pastyme of Pleasure* (1509) to denote the selection of arguments or topics; it had, of course, been in common use in Latin for this signification. A contemporary sense of its importance is provided in the printer's recommendation to the reader of 1554 as a poem "containing and treating upon the seven liberal sciences and the whole of man's life"—for which the art of rhetoric was

of enquiry. There was the question of "stances" or "issues" by which the problem might be attacked (compare the Latin *status,* with its dominating legal sense, as well as the term *constitutio),* and there was the fourfold distinction of Hermagoras: *coniectura, finis, qualitas,* and *translatio.* One significance which I should like to stress is that such meticulous analysis was valuable in training both those working in judicial oratory, the advocates and plead-ers, and those engaged in close study of text and speeches; howev-er, as D. A. F. M. Russell has observed in the *Oxford Classical Dictionary,*[4] this kind of analysis could lead (as it did later) into barren, scholastic complexities. But always the affinity between law and rhetoric existed.

In the carrying over of Greek techniques and standards of rhet-oric into the Roman schools, forums, and courts, there were fur-ther developments of *inventio,* and here one must signal first the powerful influence upon subsequent developments in rhetoric (and indeed the whole of literature) of the *progymnasmata* and *declamatio—*exercises which at our peril we think of as sterile or mechanical, for they could, under the right persuasion, train stu-

---

deemed essential. In 1531 the rhetorical sense of invention was enlarged to em-brace the signification of "contrivance or production of a new method, of an art, kind of instrument, etc. previously unknown . . . ."

It is a token of the lastingness of the symbiotic relation between law and rhetoric that in most Anglo-American jurisdictions *discovery* has meant, and in some jurisdictions is still being used to mean, that early stage in the examination of evidence by parties to action at law, or their attorneys—this is usually done by interrogation of facts relevant to the issue in the action, and within the knowledge of the party interrogated—or it may be the discovery of documents relating to matters in question in the action at hand. See *Black's Law Dictionary,* 4th rev. ed. (St. Paul, Minn.: West Publishing Co., 1968), p. 552; and *Osborn's Concise Law Dictionary,* 3rd ed. (London: Sweet & Maxwell, 1947), p. 112.

In an important contribution to the literature of legal reasoning, James L. Golden and Josina M. Makau have written "Perspectives on Judicial Reasoning," in *Exploration in Rhetoric: Studies in Honor of Douglas Ehninger,* ed. Ray E. McKerrow (Glenview, Ill.: Scott, Foresman, 1982), pp. 157–177; in this article the authors have explored the question of the invention of arguments by justices and have touched upon the role of *stare decisis* in the common law.

It is worth observing that a typical modern case book on evidence entitled *Evidence—*such as that of Edward W. Cleary and John W. Strong (St. Paul, Minn.: West Publishing Co., 1969)—totally cuts its subject from its rhetorical roots.

4. *Oxford Classical Dictionary,* 2nd ed., ed. N. G. L. Hammond and H. H. Scullard (Oxford: Clarendon Press, 1970), p. 921.

dents in the exercise of judgment, which is so much what *inventio* is all about. The other point to stress is the appropriateness of those school exercises for the society in which they were developed.

But before we leave the ancient world in such a necessarily hurried view of *inventio,* it is worth following Alain Michel in his penetrating distinction between the manual and the dialogue of rhetoric, in themselves and still more for their impact upon the art. In a paper given at the 1979 Congress of the International Association for Neo-Latin Studies in Bologna and to appear in the proceedings of that Congress, *Acta Bononiensis,* Professor Michel holds up the example of the *Phaedrus* for the one and the *Rhetorica* of Aristotle for the other tradition; and he argues that in the rhetoric which flowed from the Greeks there were fundamentally the two modes of enquiry that must be distinguished: the dialogue and the manual.

While Cicero, to be sure, wrote the manualistic *De Inventione* in his youth and the *Topica* in his late years, he in effect rejected the temptations or opportunities of the rhetorical manual in his great dialogues on rhetoric, *De Oratore* and *Orator* especially. In these dialogues we find his arguments for the complete orator as the man of wide culture who is essentially good—the position of Isocrates in countering the more glittering appeal of Gorgias. The immense influence of Cicero upon the history of rhetoric comes in large part through the dialogues, even while *De Inventione* and the pseudo-Ciceronian *Rhetorica Ad Herennium* continued for centuries as school textbooks. For the medieval traditions of rhetoric by and large stressed the manual; by contrast, the Renaissance traditions—at least until Ramus (and with few notable exceptions earlier)—favored the dialogue; and much of the spirit, if not the substance, of the great flowering of the rhetorical tradition during the Renaissance is governed by that difference. Yet I would like to expand a little more on Ciceronian influence during the Renaissance, for it has been misunderstood: as we may see in the fertility of the genre of the Ciceronian dialogue as employed by Petrarch in *De remediis fortunae,* that most popular of his

prose works, in which Petrarch dealt with Ciceronian questions;
or in Erasmus, notably in the extraordinarily influential development of dialogue into the pedagogical but entertaining *Colloquia*
and also in the *Ciceronianus,* where in a dialogue bearing the
name of the revered Cicero, Erasmus was able to criticize excesses
of Ciceronianism; and in others as well, such as the dialogues of
the influential educator of Strassburg, Sturm, or the schoolteacher
of Strassburg, Frischlin, who wrote academic plays to teach and
to delight (and in one of which Cicero is gently spoofed for failing
to understand the printing press)—in all of these, the method or
style of Cicero is not simply imitated but rather employed, adapted,
to deal directly with a wide range of intellectual, academic, and
social problems. Some of this has been dealt with by Marc Fumaroli in his recent book on Ciceronian influence in France.[5]

   Writing not during the political turbulence of the late Republic
as was Cicero, but in the relative stability of the early Empire,
Quintilian did not have to justify the place of rhetoric or to engage
in special pleading: he had inherited the teaching of Cicero, and,
as M. L. Clarke has recently shown, he extolled Cicero as the voice
of eloquence itself.[6] Quintilian's treatise derived from his own full
experience in the law courts, as a teacher of rhetoric, and (as we
might put it) as a research scholar in rhetoric after his retirement,
when he wrote up his lectures; throughout, his aim, very largely,
was to train speakers for the law courts and public life. His rhetoric therefore was eminently practical in its orientation; he stressed
that the first essential of a perfect orator was that he be a good man
(thus following Cato's definition, *vir bonus dicendi peritus*). Quintilian was practical in the educational sections of his *Institute,*
being intensely concerned with practicalities of language and usage
and always mindful of the public service to which rhetorical training would lead. His *Institutio oratoria,* or *Education of the Orator,*
is the fullest Latin rhetorical treatise that we have. It is a manual

   5. Marc Fumaroli, *L'Age de l'Eloquence: Rhetorique et res literaria de la
Renaissance au seuil de l'époque classique* (Geneva, 1980).
   6. See Martin L. Clarke's essay in *Cicero,* ed. T. A. Dorey (London: Routledge
and Kegan Paul, 1965), and his *Rhetoric at Rome* (London: Cohen and West, 1953).

that sets forth a complete theory of invention, arrangement, style, memory, and delivery in that conventional order, and it presents its theory in great detail. Quintilian's formulation or synthesis exercised such a profound influence upon the Church Fathers and the Christian schools not simply because of the scope or impressive detail of his manual, but because of the reasonableness of Quintilian himself, for as George Kennedy rightly summarizes the force of the writer, "Quintilian is above all a patient, moderate, reasonable man, dedicated to good teaching, clear thinking, and natural expression."[7]

When we look at the diverse schools of the Middle Ages—notarial, cathedral, bishops', monastic, and others—we can understand that it was the practical influence of Quintilian that was put to service in these schools along with the Ciceronian moral argument for the goodness of the orator and the high place of rhetoric as philosophy; and to these twinned traditions, so often reinforcing rather than opposing one another, we must add the influence of Augustine's theory of the Christian orator in the *De Doctrina Christiana,* where may be perceived a fusion of the interests of the young Augustine in both Platonism and Ciceronianism. Later in the Middle Ages there were specializations of the larger missions of rhetoric into several kinds: the prescriptive treatments of grammar, the *artes poetriae;* the manuals of letter writing, the *artes dictaminis;* and the arts of preaching, the *artes praedicandi;* but throughout the changes, there was an essential continuity of teaching the doctrine of the manuals of classical rhetoric, especially the *Ad Herennium,* Aristotle's *Rhetorica,* and the *De Inventione.* And one must stress the point that the force of the medieval commentaries on these last three works is only recently becoming known: witness the two-volume Toronto dissertation (1972) of John O. Ward on the *De Inventione* and *Ad Herennium.*

One focal point is to be found in the teaching traditions of the

7. George Kennedy, *Classical Rhetoric and Its Christian and Secular Tradition from Ancient to Modern Times* (Chapel Hill: University of North Carolina Press, 1970), p. 101.

32   *Richard J. Schoeck*

School of Chartres, and the commentary of Thierry of Chartres in the middle of the twelfth century can be signaled out, since it exemplifies the fusion of teaching traditions and comes at a moment of great import for Western culture—the acceleration of literacy on which Brian Stock has recently written with great acumen.[8] Thierry brought his reading of Cicero, Quintilian, Boethius, and others to bear upon his work of commenting upon Cicero's work. A major point of emphasis must be Thierry's use of the authority of Boethius to reaffirm "Cicero's dictum that rhetoric is an art which is a major part of civil science or politics."[9] Thierry of Chartres was obviously a Chartrian; his contemporary Ailred, abbot of Rielvaux, was not connected with Chartres, yet he also manifests the influence of Cicero in ways that bear upon our central concerns with rhetoric as a practical art and with *inventio* as an example, especially in his use of the dialogue form to explore and relate.[10]

We have been looking at the twelfth century; in the thirteenth century there was the rapid rise of the universities and the phenomenal development of medieval logic and theology. It is therefore not surprising that the thirteenth century has recently been declared "something of a low point for classical rhetoric in many parts of Europe, despite the recovery of Aristotle's *Rhetoric* in Latin translation at that time."[11] Once again we see that rhetoric has responded to the needs of society at a particular historical moment, and the role and consequently the interpretation of rhetoric were shaped accordingly to make it propaedeutic to and a handmaiden of dialectic and theology.

This has been a rapid survey, and I have ignored such significant contributions as that of Martianus Capella and of later encyclopedists in shaping the concept of the liberal arts as well as that of the canon. It is interesting to observe that even when the parts of

8. Brian Stock, *Myth and Science in the Twelfth Century* (Princeton, N.J.: Princeton University Press, 1972).
9. James J. Murphy, *Rhetoric in the Middle Ages* (Berkeley: University of California Press, 1974), p. 119.
10. Clarke in *Cicero*, p. 89.
11. Kennedy, p. 174.

a whole are all transmitted, the sense of that whole may be radically modified. Even while Boethius repeats that there are the five traditional parts of rhetoric (invention, arrangement, style, memory, and delivery)—I am thinking here of the fourth book of the *De Topicis Differentiis*—he has rather neatly subordinated the whole study of rhetoric to dialectic, and that subordination continues until the very late medieval period, when the revival of certain classical works by the early humanists (the discovery in 1416 of the complete text of Quintilian and at the same period the rediscovery of works of Cicero) combined to reorder the place of rhetoric in the scheme of things once again. Another kind of example can be found in the early eighth century; Bede's *De Schematibus et Tropis* is a notable little book whose entire purpose is to prepare for the study of the Bible, and so in place of conventional illustrations from classical literature Bede substitutes biblical examples. Through Bede's influence the thrust of rhetoric is that of serving the Christian preacher, and the functions of invention and authority are consequently different.

Even in so rapid a survey one must call attention to Alcuin's charming dialogue between Charlemagne and himself, both because it is a dialogue and important in continuing that tradition, but also because it proceeds from Charlemagne's establishment at the outset that the strength of the art of rhetoric lies entirely in dealing with civil questions.[12] Above all, the dialogue indicates the continuing force of Ciceronian influence. In the Carolingian empire there was a vital place for rhetoric, which continued in the new stirrings in the cities of Gaul and northern Italy, where once again the teaching of rhetoric gathered strength.

The great changeover took place with the development of the universities in the twelfth and thirteenth centuries, especially at Bologna, Paris, and Oxford, with their twin movements stressing dialectic and theology; thanks largely to Abelard, logic became the primary tool for the new theology, and thanks to the use of Boethius's *De Topicis* instead of the works of Cicero, dialectic became

12. Ibid., p. 183.

the prime tool. In place of Ciceronian dialogues we find new manuals for preaching, letter writing and poetics, and of course the disputation and quodlibet. Given the relationship of the university to its society—a society that in theory at least placed the study of the Bible, *lectio divina,* at the pinnacle of the educational scheme, making grammar and rhetoric propaedeutic to Biblical study, and gave to theology the highest valuation as the queen of the sciences—it is not surprising that logic should have dominated in place of rhetoric and that the role of *inventio* should be seen as a function of dialectic rather than rhetoric.

To perform a strategic movement of regrouping: it cannot be too much emphasized (as I have argued elsewhere in commenting upon the hypothetical typology of J. J. Murphy) that there are a number of traditions of rhetoric in the patristic and medieval ages—not simply four. Even these four are not always sharply differentiated, for at times the Horatian and the Ciceronian, for example, come together, and there were transmitting agents like Boethius, whose work cannot be accounted for entirely within a single tradition.[13] In Boethius there is a complex interplay of logic, philosophy, and rhetoric which cannot be described briefly or simply, and his influence parallels that of Augustine continuously through the Middle Ages and into the Renaissance. Besides, the milieux of educational institutions and diverse societies within the Western world, within which rhetoric was taught and called upon to serve, continued to change, and the manual that served a Carolingian court school was no longer appropriate for a monastic school three or four centuries later, nor for a humanistic establishment such as those of Guarino and Da Feltre in the fifteenth century; still more, as the Greek sources of rhetoric began to be known firsthand once again, the relationships changed accordingly.

The example of George of Trebizond provides a focus for this generalizing. His impact was a major one in the bringing of the Greek classics to the West during the fifteenth century and, for the

13. See my discussion in "On Rhetoric in Fourteenth-Century Oxford," *Mediaeval Studies* 30 (1968): 214-225.

rhetorical tradition, particularly in expanding the teaching of rhetoric that had concentrated so heavily on the Ciceronian tradition, as much through commentaries as through manuals, as we have seen. For Trebizond's masterwork drew not only from Cicero and Quintilian, but also from Hermogenes, Dionysius, and a few other Greek sources.[14] Published in 1433 or 1434, Trebizond's *Rhetoric* was widely used for a century, in manuscripts first and then in a series of printed editions; it is one of the few rhetorical works to bridge the ages of the manuscript and printed book. Kennedy notes that Vives cited Trebizond twice alongside classical authorities and that Trebizond was the only modern so honored.[15] But with the new wave of translations and critical editions, Cicero, the *Ad Herennium,* and Quintilian took the lead, along with such new texts as Erasmus's *De Copia* and his other texts for students and teachers.

What we have begun to recognize generally is that in the time of Trebizond rhetoric received—or began to receive, for university curricula and teaching habits have always changed slowly—a place in the liberal arts curriculum that roughly paralleled its place in antiquity. Much of this change was due to the example, the prestige, and the critical essays and treatises of Erasmus, as Craig R. Thompson has pointed out in his introduction to volumes 23 and 24 of the *Collected Works of Erasmus.*[16]

But Trebizond was not an isolated example: the fifteenth century witnessed, as we have seen, the discovery of the complete text of Quintilian and a fresh study of Cicero; Barzizza, appointed professor of rhetoric at Padua in 1407, expounded not only Cicero's letters, but also the *De Oratore, De Senectute,* and *De Amicitia,* paving the way for the Renaissance extolling of Cicero the philosopher. Vittorino da Feltre, one of the great educators of the Renaissance, was a pupil of Barzizza, and the humanistic concept of education of the whole person was developed as well as Ciceronian rhetoric by da Feltre and Guarino; and their influence is to be found in Castiglione's *Courtier*. The tradition of the Ciceronian dialogue continued in Cortesi's *De Hominibus Doctrina* (c. 1490), which followed Cicero's *De Legibus*, and these and other humanists contributed to the practical cast of More's *Utopia*. But Vasoli and others have studied the role of Cicero and the explorations of *inventio* in the Renaissance, and I lack the time for dealing with this question here. I would end this *narratio* by reminding you of Erasmus's fine tribute in the *Ciceronianus* where he asks

Where is Cicero's soul, where his copious and happy powers of invention . . . where finally is that mind which still breathes in his writings, that genius which brings a peculiar and secret energy?[17]

One might look past the eighteenth-century figures like Burke and Gibbon, who were in fact products of a rhetorically-oriented, humanistic education, to the nineteenth-century Newman, who in a Dublin lecture on literature defended Cicero against charges of pretentiousness and artificiality. For Newman himself was perhaps the finest example of the Ciceronian *humanus* in nineteenth-century England—Ciceronian *humanus* rather than Renaissance *humanista*—far more, I think, than Macaulay. In a celebrated passage on university education in those Dublin lectures, Newman wrote as follows:

It is the education which gives a man a clear conscious view of his own opinions and judgments, a truth in developing them, an eloquence in expressing them, and a force in urging them . . . . It prepares him to fill any post with credit, and to master any subject with facility.[18]

The theme and the faith in rhetoric and humanism are unmistakably Ciceronian, but Newman's underscoring of the ultimate utility or practicality of that education strikes a fresh note because of the nineteenth-century context and Newman's own unique power in restating that faith.

17. *Opera Omnia*, ed. Jean Le Clerc, 10 vols. in 11 (Leiden, 1703–06), I: 989.
18. John Henry Newman, *Idea of a University* (London: Longman's, 1931), p. 101.

Conclusion

Curtius has already summarized an historical case for rhetoric in writing that " . . . down to the Revolution of 1830, Europe remained convinced that it could not do without a constantly renewed presentation of rhetoric which should keep pace with contemporary literary production."[19] The historical case presented by Curtius also anticipates the argument for literary history and criticism—namely, that down to Dickens and a handful of others in the nineteenth century every major writer had received a classical education, which had at its core a rhetorical training. The implications of that for our reading and understanding of pre-twentieth century writing are enormous, as they are for our understanding the break between pre-World War II literature and what one of my colleagues has called the "Post-Contemporary."

In Curtius' formulation the operative words are "a constantly renewed presentation": unfortunately, too much of rhetoric was left in the hands of those school teachers who wanted to harden disputed questions into dogma, who wanted to preserve unchanged their long-outdated manuals. As Thomas More wrote in 1515, again quoting from his letter to Martin Dorp, "A conviction that is first handed on by stupid teachers and then strengthened in the course of years is extremely capable of perverting the judgment of even sound minds."[20]

One of our purposes in these essays is to insure that there will be a renewed presentation that will keep pace with contemporary literary production: what is arrived at, or at least reached for, must relate to the literature of our own age, and it must be of service for all of those writing needs that we are so acutely conscious of now or can anticipate for tomorrow. Three and a half centuries ago the Académie Française was charged with producing not only a dictionary and a grammar (which it did), but also

19. Curtius, p. 78.
20. *Selected Letters,* p. 20.

a rhetoric and a poetics (which it did not); Curtius reminds us of that multiple charge, and one might add the reflection that the dynamics of a rhetoric and a poetics might have contributed to a greater or longer life in the grammar and perhaps might even have obviated some of the Barthesian and Deconstructive rebellion against linguistic norms that one finds in France today, and which some of our students and colleagues find so attractive.

But our role in America is surely that of generating out of the inexhaustible resources of classical rhetoric, when studied under the proper persuasion, a rhetoric for our times in our culture, and not an anti-rhetoric or a non-rhetoric. There have been revolts before: in the sixteenth century the work of Peter Ramus was fundamentally anti-rhetoric, though ironically he held a chair of rhetoric in Paris. Like Agricola's dialectic in the preceding century, Ramistic rhetoric included invention, and the reduction both of the importance of rhetoric generally and the transfer of invention to the domain of dialectic may be taken as an indication that Ramus was not primarily training orators, like Quintilian, or writers, but rather schoolboys who could become in turn teachers of tropes and figures and be able to write a Latin that was distinctively modern. Ramism was also anti-Aristotelian, and it was a part of the revolt of the sixteenth century against traditional authority of more than one kind; Ramism can also be compared to the work of a deconstructionist like Barthes; and like the work of Barthes it had a wide appeal, both in Latin and in the vernacular, ranging from Gabriel Harvey and Abraham Fraunce to even less known writers like Charles Butler, and it was a considerable influence, as Rosemond Tuve has persuasively argued, upon Elizabethan and metaphysical imagery.[21]

It will doubtless already have been inferred by many of you that my theory of rhetoric is a humanistic one. To follow for a moment Ernesto Grassi's deeply perceptive essay on rhetoric as a basis for philosophic thought (an approach further developed in other books

21. Rosemond Tuve, *Elizabethan and Metaphysical Imagery: Renaissance Poetic and Twentieth Century Critics* (Chicago: University of Chicago Press, 1947).

by younger colleagues at Munich, Eckhard Kessler and Hanna Barbara Gerl), it can be manifestly and coherently argued that rhetoric rather than scientific thought is the sounder ground for society and its deeper needs, and that this humanistic view breaks with the mathematical ideal of knowledge.[22] The long tradition for this humanist view is vigorously presented by Grassi: from Latini and Dante (based largely on Cicero and his concept of rhetoric as philosophy, developed in his dialogues far more than in his manuals), and from Dante and Petrarch and thus to the humanistic developments of Landino and Bruni, and Valla in the fourteenth century. Leonardo Bruni, finding the scholastic language of his day inadequate for translating such Greek texts as the *Nicomachean Ethics,* recognized that "language originates in the different situations in which human beings interact with reality," and he stressed "the primacy of language's historical character, dialectic, and topics."[23]

Rational speech, which especially when combined with mathematical symbols is the domain of logic and science, is of course important, and the explanation of and the inferences drawn from observed data cannot be ignored nor their importance diminished; nor would humanists want to minimize that great contribution to modern society. But we cannot allow the concept of the mathematical model to dominate our own explorations of the functions of language or the role of rhetoric in operating within the dynamics of language and reality. In his well-known essay entitled "The Retreat from the Word" (in *Language and Silence*), as Edward Corbett has already summarized it for us,[24] George Steiner "paints a gloomy picture of how academically respectable disciplines such as chemistry, physics, biology, history, and economics are recording and transmitting their knowl-

22. *Rhetoric as Philosophy: The Humanistic Tradition* (University Park: Pennsylvania State University Press, 1980).
23. Ibid., p. 91.
24. Edward P. J. Corbett summarizes Steiner in "Rhetoric Whither Goest Thou?" *Rhetoric and Change,* ed. William E. Tanner and J. Dean Bishops (Mesquite, Tex.: Ide House, 1982), p. 17 .

edge, not in articulated sentences but in the mathematical modes of the chart, the graph, the curve, and the statistical table. What has happened, Steiner says, is that 'the sum of realities of which words can give a necessary and sufficient account has sharply diminished'. . . ." Not only has the sum of realities of which words can give account diminished, but the view of reality has inexorably been changing as it more and more leaves out that which words provide account for.

An emphasis on the role of rhetoric and a questioning of the mathematical model as the only model are the more urgently needed—together with the perception and conviction to be gained from the verbal model—as we move farther and with accelerating pace into a conceptual world in which the cry for computer literacy is heard throughout the land and verbal literacy all but ignored. A notable exception is the analysis of the high school report just published by the Carnegie Foundation for the Advancement of Teaching. This report swims against the current of calls for more science and mathematics, and it urges greater emphasis on the mastery of English, writing and critical thinking. An editorial in the *New York Times* (September 25, 1983), entitled "Education for a 'Transformed World'," underscores the need for verbal literacy and analytical thought; education, the *Times* editorial concludes, best serves the economy by teaching people to think, to communicate, and to understand their world.

Finally, rhetoric is more than a practical art and, as I suggested earlier, one of the oldest professions. As Grassi reminds us, rhetorical speech exists and is continually reborn at the end of a long and living tradition that connects us with Cicero in our own time; rhetorical speech is fundamentally a dialogue: it is the use of language which comes into being in response to human needs, which is born out of the urgencies of a particular human situation in a moment of history, which forms uniquely the expression and discovers the necessary means and form for the confrontation of human beings with other human beings and then moves through language and rhetoric toward understanding each of the other. This use of language is a precious gift for man *qua* human being—

not laboratory animal, nor computer statistic—and it cannot be sacrificed to other concepts of reality, to other systems dedicated purely to efficiency; nor may we ourselves within the citadel of language and rhetoric permit rhetoric to be taken over by semiotics or linguistics (useful tools though they unquestionably are, provided that they remain for us servants and not masters); nor, still less, may we allow rhetoric to be understood only as an art of decoration, or even a practical art of persuasion, if it is restricted to being only that.

Edward P. J. Corbett

3 The *Topoi* Revisited

In the last ten years or so, teachers of writing have concentrated a remarkable amount of attention on invention or heuristics. Even so, this preoccupation with the discovery process has not yet equalled the interest of contemporary scholars in style, that other important canon of classical rhetoric. But the extent and the depth of the attention given to invention have been considerable. Richard Leo Enos and some of his colleagues at Carnegie-Mellon University compiled a listing that they entitled "Heuristic Procedures and the Composing Process: A Selected Bibliography" and published it in a special issue of the *Rhetoric Society Quarterly* in 1982. They grouped their listings under fifteen categories, and although one could question the pertinence of some of their categories to the general subject of heuristics, they did come up with a total of 679 entries, most of which were published between 1970 and 1980.

Why this sudden resurgence of interest in the canon of rhetoric to which the classical rhetoricians devoted most of their teaching? There are certainly a number of reasons for that resurgence, but one of those reasons must be the renewed emphasis that teachers of writing have given recently to the *process* of composing. If you are interested in the process of writing, you have to be interested in how writers find or invent what they are going to say.

There has always been a lively interest among teachers and students of creative writing in how novelists, for instance, "invent" their characters and their plots. The most frequently asked question of novelists on talk shows is "Where do you get your ideas for your stories?" One would expect conscious artists to have ready answers to a question like that, but curiously enough, novelists and short story writers have not been very illuminating about how they create their fictions. If you read the interviews with contemporary fiction writers that were published in the *Paris Review,* you will be surprised at how little these writers say about their creative process. They talk all around the question but never zero in on it. They will give you nuts-and-bolts information about how they have to sharpen all their pencils before they begin the day's work and have to write on yellow legal pads, but they never really get down to telling you how they create their stories.

One suspects that novelists are reluctant to give out the secrets of their craft lest other writers appropriate those secrets and become serious rivals. The truth of the matter is more likely to be that most of them have never been introspective enough about the process of their craft to discover how they go about doing what they can do superlatively well. One novelist that came close to giving out his trade secrets was Henry James. At times in his *Notebooks,* he gave us amazingly precise and detailed information about how the "germ" of a story evolved into the full-blown story that we read today.

It has been only since the shift of interest from the finished product to the generating process that many teachers of composition have developed a curiosity about how their students go about writing the papers that they are assigned to write. Teachers have made deliberate efforts to observe their students in the act of writing, to question them about their writing habits, and to speculate about their cognitive processes from analyzing the revisions that they make from draft to draft. Janet Emig received quite a bit of notoriety for doing what sociologists had been doing for a long time: developing case studies of the writing practices of a group of high school students. Linda Flower had students talking into tape recorders while in the act of writing. Students have been videotaped while composing a paper, and they have written with electronic pens so that their stops and starts could be recorded and tabulated. In trying to plumb the mystery of the composing process, English teachers have been receiving lots of help from psychologists and psycholinguists. In the articles on composition appearing in our professional journals, it is common now for us to read about learning theory and hemisphericity and to encounter names like Jean Piaget, Jerome Bruner, Lev Vygotsky, A. R. Luria, and Michael Polanyi.

There is a feeling abroad among English teachers that they have come a long way in their efforts to anatomize the mental processes involved in writing and in their efforts to teach writing. I am convinced that they *are* much more sophisticated than teachers of composition were even fifteen years ago. But it would be instructive to investigate where we have come from and try to determine just how much progress we have made—if, in fact, we have made any. One way to conduct that investigation would be to trace the history of the topics in rhetorical theory and practice, examine what the *topoi* were for the Greek rhetoricians, review the modifications, extensions, and innovations that later rhetoricians made, and then try to assess where we are today in relation to the tradition.

Aristotle seems not to have been the originator of the notion of the *topoi*. The notion was in the air when he wrote his *Rhetoric*. He merely picked it up and, as he usually did, impressed it with his own stamp. For him and for his contemporaries, the *topoi* were devices enabling the speaker to find those arguments that would be most persuasive in a given situation. Aristotle classified the topics into two main kinds: the common topics (*koinoi topoi*) and the special topics (*eidē*).

It would have helped us all if, having made that classification, Aristotle had given us an explicit definition of both kinds of topics. He may have given such definitions in his lectures on rhetoric to his students, but if he ever wrote such definitions for his *Rhetoric,* they have not survived in the extant text. We can construct definitions by inference from what he says about them in his rhetoric text. And down through the ages various commentators have invented alternate terminology for the *topoi,* have formulated their definitions of the kinds of *topoi,* and have offered their own interpretations of these heuristic devices. We can fairly safely infer that the common topics were devices to find arguments for writing or speaking on any subject whatsoever but that the special topics were devices for finding arguments appropriate to a particular kind of discourse. In Chapters 4 through 14 of the First Book of the *Rhetoric,* Aristotle dealt with the special topics pertinent to deliberative oratory, epideictic oratory, and forensic oratory, respectively. He first mentions the common topics in Chapter 2, but he treats at some length of four common topics in Chapter 19 of the Second Book: (1) Possible and Impossible, (2) Past Fact and Future Fact, (3) Greatness and Smallness, (4) Amplification and Depreciation. But he muddies the waters a bit when in Chapter 23 of the same book, he treats of twenty-eight common topics. One wonders whether there could be that many common topics yielding arguments for virtually any subject.

William M. A. Grimaldi may have given the explanation that can dissipate our wonder.[1] He groups the twenty-eight topics into just three categories: (1) Antecedent-Consequent or Cause-Effect, (2) More-Less, and (3) Some Form of Relation. That kind of reduction by grouping gives these topics more of the air of the general or universal that we associate with the common topics. In that same article, he makes a very illuminating distinction between the special or particular topics and the common topics. He says that the special topics yield *subject matter* or *content* for arguments and that the common topics represent *patterns* or *forms* of inference. More than any other explanation of the topics, Grimaldi's distinction helps us to see why the common topics can

---

1. William M. A. Grimaldi, S.J., "The Aristotelian *Topics," Traditio* 14 (1958): 1–16. Reprinted in *Aristotle: The Classical Heritage of Rhetoric,* ed. Keith V. Erickson (Metuchen, N.J.: Scarecrow Press, 1974), pp. 176–193.

be used in dealing with any subject, whereas the special topics are tied to a particular kind of discourse.

What eventually emerges from Aristotle's sometimes murky treatment of the topics, both special and common, is that they represent a head or genus under which many rhetorical arguments are grouped (Book II, Chapter 26). The topics are, to use W. Rhys Roberts's term, "lines of argument," and their classification is based on the characteristic ways in which the human mind reasons or thinks. For me, the notion that the topics represent the natural way in which the human mind reasons or thinks keeps the topics from being some kind of artificial gimmick that the ancient rhetoricians invented to facilitate the thinking process—a kind of "thinking by the numbers." Just as the syllogism represented Aristotle's systemization of how the human mind reasons deductively, the topics represented Aristotle's codification of the various ways in which the human mind probes a subject to discover something significant or cogent that can be said about that subject.

The Latin rhetoricians picked up on the notion of the topics and, as we have been shown by scholars like Elbert W. Harrington and Michael C. Leff, put their own distinctive stamp on the topics.[2] They preserved the notion that the topics were *places* that one consulted to find suitable arguments by using the Latin word *loci* as the equivalent of the Greek word *topoi*. That metaphor of *places* is preserved in some of the other images that rhetoricians like Cicero and Quintilian used when referring to the topics: "seats (*sedes*)," "regions," "veins or mines," "storehouses or thesauri." One of the common extended metaphors that the Latin rhetoricians used was that of the hunter who stalked the haunts of certain wild game, knowing that he would be likely to find his prey there. So the Latin rhetoricians preserved the notion of the topics as

2. Elbert W. Harrington, *Rhetoric and the Scientific Method of Inquiry: A Study of Invention,* University of Colorado Studies in Language and Literature, No. 1 (Boulder, Colo.: 1948); and Michael C. Leff, "The Topics of Argumentative Invention in Latin Rhetorical Theory from Cicero to Boethius," *Rhetorica* 1 (Spring 1983): 23–44.

finding devices, but little else did they preserve of the notion of the topics as they appropriated it from Aristotle. For one thing, the special or particular topics disappeared in the rhetorics of Cicero and Quintilian—at least the term and the concept disappeared. For another thing, the Latin topics were never expressed in the form of propositions, as they sometimes were in Aristotle. Whereas Aristotle sometimes posed his special and common topics in the form of such axiomatic sentences as "What is rare is a greater good than what is plentiful" (Book I, Chapter 7) and "If a quality does not in fact exist where it is more likely to exist, it clearly does not exist where it is less likely" [the *a fortiori* principle] (Book II, Chapter 23), the topics in the Latin rhetorics invariably bear single-word or phrasal labels such as *definition, similarity, dissimilarity, contraries, contradictions, antecedent and consequence, cause and effect.* Thirdly, the topics in the Latin rhetorics were all devoted to discovering the matter or the content of arguments and never, as they sometimes were in Aristotle, to the inferential form of arguments.[3] Fourthly, the Latin *loci communes* were often not the equivalent of the Greek common topics (*koinoi topoi*); rather they were set pieces, stored away for future incorporation into a speech when the need for such arguments presented itself. These ready-made arguments were the inspiration for the so-called commonplace books that Renaissance schoolboys were later required to keep.

Although the Latin rhetoricians appropriated the Greek system of the topics and impressed it with their own stamp, they hardly advanced the discipline of the topics. Both Cicero and Quintilian advocated a reliance on the fruits of a liberal education more than on the mechanism of a topical system. Quintilian especially thought of the topics as a valuable training device for callow pupils aspiring to be eloquent orators, but it is clear that he hoped the maturi-

3. However, Donovan J. Ochs contends that some of Cicero's *topica* were concerned with the formal structure of argument. See his article "Cicero's *Topica:* A Process View of Invention," in *Explorations in Rhetoric: Studies in Honor of Douglas Ehninger,* ed. Ray E. McKerrow (Glenview, Ill.: Scott, Foresman, 1982), pp. 107–118.

ty that came with experience and formal education would wean the pupils away from this rather mechanical system of heuristics.

Not only did rhetoric take a subordinate position to grammar and logic in the medieval trivium, but the topics seem to have changed their complexion altogether. In treating the topics in Chapter Five of his great book *European Literature and the Latin Middle Ages*, Ernst Robert Curtius shows that they became not so much devices for finding persuasive arguments in letter writing (*ars dictaminis*) and preaching (*ars praedicandi*) as guiding principles for the composition of literary texts.[4] The topics became not so much sources of arguments as suggesters of common themes or conventions in literary texts. For instance, for funeral sermons or for letters of condolence, there was an elaborate formula of consolatory discourse. Stereotyped themes crept into these messages: "All men must eventually die"; "Even famous, powerful men have died"; "Even young men in the prime of their life have died." New *topoi* were developed which in turn spawned other sets of hackneyed themes and conventions in poetry. For instance, for the introduction of a long poem, the convention developed of the poet affecting modesty. Topics devised for the conclusions of long poems created the convention of abrupt endings, justified by a trite insistence on the theme of weariness. There were the recurrent themes of the "upside-down world," the "aged boy," and the "youthful woman." These new *topoi* served to formularize literature but did little to enliven or innovate it. Even with Boethius's *De differentiis topicis*, a popular and influential text of the sixth century, we do not get much of a revitalization of the topics. Boethius did revive Aristotle's notion of the topics as forms of inference, but ultimately he was more interested in creating a coherent art of the topics than in developing a topical system that could be used in practical arguments.

The study of rhetoric became vigorous and influential once

---

4. Ernst Robert Curtius, *European Literature and the Latin Middle Ages*, trans. Willard R. Trask, Bollingen Series, 36 (Princeton, N.J.: Princeton University Press, 1953), pp. 79–105.

again in the Renaissance schools, but interest in the topics began to fade.[5] The topics continued to be taught in the schools, of course, and the system that was adopted was largely that of the Latin rhetoricians. But there were no real innovations in topical theory, and with the growing ascendancy of John Locke's empiricism, speakers and writers in the "real world" began to rely on a more scientific epistemic system to discover matter for their discourses. There was a widespread revolt, especially in the eighteenth century, against the epistemology practiced by the so-called scholastic philosophers, and the syllogism became the symbol of the mode of thinking that the Age of Reason was rejecting. Associated with that medieval mode of deductive reasoning, the topics were not only rejected by the intelligentsia but also ridiculed. It is worth quoting at length what Hugh Blair said about the topics in Lecture 32 of the series he delivered for twenty-four years at the University of Edinburgh. The views of this popular teacher of rhetoric are typical of the reactionary attitude to the heuristic system that had reigned in the schools for centuries. Here is what Blair said:

> The Grecian sophists were the first inventors of this artificial system of oratory; and they showed a prodigious subtlety and fertility in the contrivance of these *loci*. Succeeding rhetoricians, dazzled by the plan, wrought them up into so regular a system that one would think they meant to teach how a person might mechanically become an orator without any genius at all. They gave him recipes for making speeches on all manner of subjects. At the same time, it is evident that though this study of commonplaces might produce very showy academical declamations, it could never produce discourses on real business. The *loci* indeed supplied a most exuberant fecundity of matter. One who had no other aim but to talk copiously and plausibly, by consulting them on every subject and laying hold of all that they suggested, might discourse without end; and that, too, though he had none but the most superficial knowledge of his subject. But such discourse could be no other than triv-

5. For a full treatment of the use of "commonplaces" in the Renaissance period, see Sister Joan Marie Lechner, *Renaissance Concepts of the Commonplaces: An Historical Investigation of the General and Universal Ideas Used in All Argumentation and Persuasion, with Special Emphasis on the Educational and Literary Tradition of the Sixteenth and Seventeenth Centuries* (New York: Pageant Press, 1962).

ial. What is truly solid and persuasive must be drawn "*ex visceribus causae*" ["from the very bowels of the case"], from a thorough knowledge of the subject and profound meditation on it. They who would direct students of oratory to any other sources of argumentation only delude them; and by attempting to render rhetoric too perfect an art, they render it, in truth, a trifling and childish study.[6]

Blair's depreciation of the topics could stand as an articulation of the reasons many teachers today have declined to use this heuristic system in the composition classroom. In their view, the topics are unduly complicated, stifle creativity, and produce dull, trivial discourse. In this rejection of the topics, there is a hint of the Romantic revolt against system and formula, a mood that helps to account for the fading of rhetoric from the curricula of the schools during the first three-quarters of the nineteenth century. Ultimately, this view led to the educational tenet that writing could not really be taught and that all the writing teacher could do in the classroom was to teach the students some editing skills.

Richard Young contends that those who have adopted the Romantic spirit of revulsion against system have failed to make the distinction between rule-governed procedures and heuristic procedures.[7] Rule-governed procedures, he says, set forth a finite series of steps, which, if followed exactly, will invariably produce the desired results. The set of instructions that the manufacturer provides for the assembly of the baby's crib we buy at the department store is an example of a rule-governed procedure. A heuristic procedure, on the other hand, sets forth, as Young explains, "a series of questions or operations whose results are provisional" but that increase our efficiency in gathering data. The classical topics and the tagmemic system, which Young espouses, are two examples of a heuristic procedure.

With the revival of interest in rhetoric and invention in the

6. Hugh Blair, *Lectures on Rhetoric and Belles Lettres* (1783), quoted from *The Rhetoric of Blair, Campbell, and Whately*, ed. James L. Golden and Edward P. J. Corbett (New York: Holt, Rinehart and Winston, 1980). p. 118.

7. Richard Young, "Invention: A Topographical Survey," in *Teaching Composition: 10 Bibliographical Essays*, ed. Gary Tate (Fort Worth: Texas Christian University, 1976), p. 2.

mid-sixties, a number of heuristic procedures were proposed as supplements or alternatives to the classical topics. One of those systems was the nine-cell grid of heuristic probes developed by Richard Young, Alton Becker, and Kenneth Pike from a union of the three perspectives from physics—particle, wave, and field—and the three perspectives from tagmemic linguistics—contrast, range of variation, and distribution. This method, according to Young, was designed to help the writer carry out three productive activities when faced with a problematic situation: "retrieval of relevant information already known, analysis of problematic data, and discovery of ordering principles." "It is also designed," he said, "to help one discover features of the audience which facilitate communication."[8]

What Richard Young suggests here about the function of the tagmemic system of invention, most fully presented in the textbook *Rhetoric: Discovery and Change* by Young, Becker, and Pike, could be adopted as the program for any of the heuristic procedures that have been devised. In the essay from which the above quotation was taken, "Invention: A Topographical Survey," in *Teaching Composition: 10 Bibliographical Essays,* Richard Young has discussed what he considers to be the four major methods of invention that have emerged in the twentieth century—neo-classical invention, Kenneth Burke's dramatistic method, D. Gordon Rohman's pre-writing, Kenneth Pike's tagmemic invention—and has specified the articles, books, and textbooks that deal with those systems. That bibliographical essay, together with the one listing current textbooks that deal with one or other of those systems of invention, a listing prepared by five former participants in one of Young's NEH seminars in rhetoric, "A Critical Survey of Resources for Teaching Rhetorical Invention: A Review Essay,"[9] would provide a good introduction for teachers of

8. Young, p. 23.
9. David V. Harrington, Philip M. Keith, Charles W. Kneupper, Janice A. Tripp, and William F. Woods, "A Critical Survey of Resources for Teaching Rhetorical Invention: A Review Essay," *College English* 40 (February 1979): 641–661. Reprinted in *The Writing Teacher's Sourcebook,* ed. Gary Tate and Edward P. J.

composition who are not yet familiar with the current techniques of invention.

Most college teachers of composition are now familiar with at least the broad outlines of those four major systems, but let me just mention the salient features of the two systems that I have not yet said anything about—Burke's dramatistic method and Rohman's pre-writing system. Burke's inventional system is an adaptation of the pentad of *act, scene, agent, agency,* and *purpose* that Burke proposed in his *A Grammar of Motives* as a device of literary analysis. As Burke said there, "Any complete statement about motives will offer some kind of answers to these five questions: what was done (*act*), when or where it was done (*scene*), who did it (*agent*), how he did it (*agency*), and why (*purpose*)."[10] The pentad looks very much like the formulaic questions that journalists were once taught to answer in the lead of any news story: *who, what, when, where, why,* and *how.* But Burke makes his system somewhat more complex when he proposes that the components of his pentad work best in combinations or, as he calls them, "ratios"—for example, *act-scene, act-purpose, act-agency.* It should be obvious that this system of generative questions is most suited to narrative kinds of discourse.

The so-called "pre-writing" system first appeared in a 1964 report by D. Gordon Rohman and Albert O. Wlecke entitled *Pre-Writing: The Construction and Application of Models for Concept Formation in Writing,* but it was made widely known to teachers of composition in Professor Rohman's article "Pre-Writing: The Stage of Discovery in the Writing Process" published the following year in *College Composition and Communication.*[11] Roh-

Corbett (New York: Oxford University Press, 1981), pp. 187–206. For a survey of the treatment of invention in fifty-seven twentieth-century rhetoric texts, see Janice M. Lauer, "Invention in Contemporary Rhetoric: Heuristic Procedures," Ph.D. diss., University of Michigan, 1967. There is an extensive bibliography on pp. 185–218 of this dissertation.

10. Kenneth Burke, *A Grammar of Motives* (New York: Prentice-Hall, 1945), p. xv.

11. D. Gordon Rohman and Albert O. Wlecke, *Pre-Writing: The Construction and Application of Models for Concept Formation in Writing,* U.S. Office of Educa-

man proposed that teachers of composition can best enable their students to become proficient writers by leading them to a "self-actualization" of their own latent powers. That self-actualization could be prodded along by various means, especially by engaging the students in the practices of keeping a journal, of concentrated thinking akin to religious meditation, and of using analogies. Of those means, the one that caught on most during the 1970s was the practice of keeping a journal, but that practice may have been prompted more by the free-writing movement of teachers like Ken Macrorie and Peter Elbow than by Rohman's pre-writing system.

A system of invention that does not fit conveniently into one of the classifications mentioned above is problem-solving. For a long time problem-solving has been a heuristic procedure in the sciences, but in recent years some authors of college rhetoric texts have adopted and adapted the procedure in composition classes. The title of Linda Flower's rhetoric text signals its orientation, *Problem-Solving Strategies for Writing.*[12] What most of the problem-solving texts do is lay out a series of steps or strategies to be followed in analyzing and solving a problem. Essentially, the sequence of steps or strategies would be somewhat like the following: (1) precisely define what the problem is that needs to be solved; (2) describe what is known for sure about the problematic situation; (3) designate the unknown in the situation, the element or elements that may hold the secret of the solution of the problem; (4) formulate a hypothesis about how to discover the unknown, which will lead to a solution of the problem; and (5) test the hypothesis for its intrinsic soundness and for its comparative merits in relation to other hypothetical solutions.

Students who are scientifically inclined often find the problem-solving procedure extremely helpful in finding something to say

tion Research Project No. 2174 (East Lansing, Mich.: Michigan State University, 1964); and D. Gordon Rohman, "Pre-Writing: The Stage of Discovery in the Writing Process," *College Composition and Communication* 16 (May 1965): 106–112.
    12. Linda Flower, *Problem-Solving Strategies for Writing* (New York: Harcourt Brace Jovanovich, 1981).

on an assigned or a chosen topic. Brainstorming is another technique that they find helpful in connection with problem-solving. Brainstorming works best with groups of people. For instance, once a problem has been defined, a whole class of students can be asked to propose, in a random and rapid-fire fashion, suggestions either about the sources of the problem or about possible solutions to the problem. Once students have some experience with brainstorming in groups, they can use it privately as a heuristic technique in a writing situation. Another technique that has been adopted from the business world and used in connection with problem-solving is the case-study approach. The case study presents a rather detailed description of a fictional or a real problematic situation in some business or industry. Once all the pertinent data have been presented, students are asked to formulate their solution to the problem and then to write a report that culminates in concrete recommendations for solving the problem. A number of teachers have testified about the effectiveness of brainstorming and case studies in conjunction with problem-solving in situations where other systems of invention have failed to be helpful to their students.

When one closely examines the heuristic systems that have been developed in this century, one notes the affinity that many of them have with the classical system of the topics. Burke's pentad, for instance, could be viewed as a version of the series of questions, like *Quis, Quid, Quando, Quomodo, Quare,* that the Latin rhetoricians used as *topoi* when discussing a particular person. The familiar methods of paragraph development that have figured so prominently in twentieth-century rhetoric texts are simply applications of some of the topics of the Latin rhetoricians, such as comparison and contrast, cause and effect, classification and division, definition, example, and testimony. The attention given in all contemporary rhetoric texts to the Use of the Library is nothing more than a form of Aristotle's nonartistic proofs. And of course in the twentieth century, we rely much more heavily on these extrinsic sources of data than did scholars in Greek and Roman times. For contemporary students of the humanities engaged in research, the library, with its thousands and thousands of books stored on row after row of shelves, is the primary source of data. In order to gain access to that thesaurus of knowledge, students must acquire some sense of what is available and of how to get at it. Once students find the sources of data, they have to extract and process what may be useful to them. Before the invention of the photocopier, students laboriously copied out by hand the pertinent notes that they had culled from the vast resources of the library. In the future, the computer will further facilitate the retrieval and recording of the pertinent data stored in this repository.

The mention of the computer suggests that we might consider what future, if any, the *topoi* may have in our educational system. It might be possible to program computers in terms of common and special *topoi*. Some indexing system analogous to the one used in *Roget's Thesaurus* or in Mortimer Adler's *Syntopicon* might be the key for electronically unlocking the teeming storehouses of knowledge. But it is not enough for us to be able to retrieve data; we must be able to select and shape the data to serve our purpose. The *formal* aspect of the *topoi* may be helpful for this marshaling process. In "A Plea for a Modern Set of *Topoi* " published some twenty years ago, Dudley Bailey suggested that a modern rhetoric should "concentrate on the sorts of logical connections between facts, things, events—whatever we call the stuff of our thoughts. And its primary task would be to consider those connections in a systematic way and to explain their logical assumptions with some thoroughness."[13] Bailey thought that for this study of the logical relations and patterns of things, we might get some help from the essays that Samuel Taylor Coleridge published in *The Friend.* But a likelier source of help might be the mental conditioning of our students that could come from their hands-on experience with the computer. Anyone who has worked with a data processor or a word processor is aware of the rigid and inexorable logic of the computer. The computer will simply not

13. *College English* 26 (November 1964): 111–117.

respond to incorrect (read "illogical") commands. Our students, who feel more comfortable with the computer than we older people do, are learning how to accommodate themselves to that kind of inexorable logic. One of the consequences of that experience, I think, is that it is going to be easier for us to train our students in the rigors and rigidities of inferential reasoning.

But inferential reasoning is more of a dialectical skill than a rhetorical skill. What seems to be more promising for the improvement of our students' rhetorical skills is the work being done in the area of artificial intelligence. A short time ago there was an interesting article in the *New York Times Magazine* about the pioneering research being done in artificial intelligence by computer scientists like Douglas R. Hofstadter of Indiana University.[14] For all of its wondrous capabilities, the computer is still not able to make some of the simple kinds of judgment and discrimination that ordinary human beings can make quite readily. For instance, computers can be programmed to "read" the account number on the face of a check if that number is printed in a certain font of type, but the computer still cannot look at an array of the letter *B* printed in a variety of sizes and formats and judge that all those configurations represent the same letter of the alphabet. But an ordinary child in first grade can make that discrimination.

Until computers can be programmed to make that kind of discrimination, they may continue to work faster and more indefatigably than people do, but they will not be "smarter" than people are. I suspect that computers will not acquire that kind of "smarts" until they develop a "topical sense." Then, and only then, will the computer become a "rhetorician," and then, and only then, will the computer become the generator of relevant ideas and arguments and proofs that the *topoi* have been for generations of speakers and writers. Then Aristotle, wherever he may be, can heave a sigh of relief and say, "I thought you'd never get here, IBM."

14. James Gleick, "Exploring the Labyrinth of the Mind," *The New York Times Magazine*, 21 August 1983, pp. 23–27, 83, 86, 87, 100.

Maxine C. Hairston

---

4 Bringing Aristotle's Enthymeme
   into the Composition Classroom

The subject of my paper is the Aristotelian enthymeme. It is the
rhetorical device that occupies a central position in Aristotle's
Rhetoric, and it is considered by some scholars to be the one
rhetorical strategy that incorporates the three major elements of
rhetoric or persuasive discourse: rational appeal, emotional appeal, and ethical appeal. Yet it is a term that one seldom encoun-
ters in current textbooks on rhetoric or in the professional literature,
and it is certainly a term that is unfamiliar to most composition
teachers. Even those teachers who are familiar with the term and
the concept because they have taken courses in classical rhetoric
are not, to my knowledge, using it in their writing classrooms.

Such neglect is rather surprising considering the prominent place
that the enthymeme holds in Aristotle's rhetorical theory. In the
Rhetoric he calls enthymemes "the very body and substance of
persuasion" and complains that the authors of previous works on
rhetoric have dwelt on "irrelevant matters" because they do not
instruct their pupils in the art of the enthymeme.¹ He goes on to

---

1. Aristotle, *The Rhetoric,* ed. Lane Cooper (New York: Appleton-Century-
Crofts, 1932), p. 1.

assert that the enthymeme is usually the most effective form of persuasion and says without qualification, "Whenever men in speaking effect persuasion through proofs, they do so either with examples or enthymemes; they use nothing else."[2] In light of such strong statements from the master himself, it does seem strange that modern scholars of rhetoric have not paid more attention to the device.

I speculate that there are probably at least three reasons the enthymeme is seldom mentioned by those working in contemporary rhetorical theory, and why, in English departments at least, it is seldom taught in composition courses. The first reason is that for centuries most people working in rhetoric, including writing teachers, seem to have misunderstood and oversimplified the enthymeme; with a few notable exceptions—and James Kinneavy and Edward Corbett are among them—scholars and teachers writing about the enthymeme have defined it in much more rigid and narrow terms than Aristotle did. Second, most faculty who teach writing have majored in literature and take no serious interest in rhetoric or its strategies, believing that it lies outside of the realm of disinterested inquiry they consider their proper area of study. Third, in the last ten or fifteen years, as more and more basic writers have entered composition programs and as the focus of teaching in those programs has shifted from product to process, formal logic has increasingly been dropped from those courses and, along with it, the enthymeme. I want to expand on all these points.

First, let's look at the ways in which the enthymeme has been misunderstood and oversimplified. Traditionally, both rhetoricians and writing teachers have defined the enthymeme as simply an abbreviated syllogism, compressed into a statement that leaves out one of the premises. For example:

Formal syllogism: All graduates of Harvard are well educated. Elaine is a Harvard graduate. Therefore she must be well educated.

2. Aristotle, p. 10.

Enthymeme: Elaine must be well educated since she graduated from Harvard.

The major premise, "All graduates of Harvard are well educated," has been omitted because the writer assumes that the audience would agree with the unstated proposition about Harvard.

Here is another example.

Syllogism: Science departments in major universities are controlled by men. Men scientists discriminate against women scientists. Therefore women scientists have trouble getting ahead in science departments in major universities.

Enthymeme: Women scientists in departments at major universities will have trouble getting ahead in their profession because their departments are controlled by men.

The premise that male scientists discriminate against women scientists is not expressed.

In each of these examples, the shortened version, or the enthymeme, saves time and effort for both the writer or speaker and the audience. Thus, the common conception of an enthymeme is that it is no more than a shorthand method for expressing a conclusion that has really been arrived at by syllogistic reasoning.

All of this seems simple enough, unlikely to cause any difficulties. Yet I think difficulties have grown up precisely because this definition is more than simple: it's simplistic. It reduces the enthymeme to little more that a convenient device and loses the rich rhetorical potential that Aristotle envisioned for it. To summarize that view, I want to draw on two important works on the enthymeme, one written almost fifty years ago by a scholar in speech communication, James McBurney, and the other written almost thirty-five years ago by a student of philosophy, William M. A. Grimaldi.

Aristotle's Conception of the Enthymeme

Both McBurney and Grimaldi stress that for Aristotle the enthymeme was the "rhetorical syllogism"; he was careful to distinguish it from the demonstrative or scientific syllogisms that philosophers and scientists use to arrive at natural laws or scientific principles. He insisted, however, that it serves the same function in rhetoric as the full, three-part logical syllogism serves in science and dialectic—that is, it links the parts of an argument together. Its form, however, is different and for good reasons. The person who undertakes to prove something with a scientific syllogism must articulate each premise and proceed carefully from major premise to minor premise to conclusion, being careful to show the audience each step in the chain of reasoning. This is Aristotle's method in the *Analytics* and other scientific works. It is also the method of dialectic that Plato uses to lead his listeners to universal truths.

Rhetoricians, however, necessarily deal with the pragmatic and the immediate, not with absolutes. Nevertheless, as Lloyd Bitzer points out, "The practical justification of rhetoric is analogous to that of scientific inquiry: the world presents objects to be known, puzzles to be resolved, complexities to be understood—hence the practical need for scientific inquiry and discourse; similarly, the world presents imperfections to be modified by means of discourse—hence the practical need for rhetorical investigation and discourse."[3] In this kind of reasoning—and it is a kind of reasoning—Aristotle says that the links in the chain must be few, for the listener will supply the missing premises that are common knowledge. Thus, Aristotle sees the enthymeme as the appropriate form of discourse when the speaker's concern is human affairs and when the speaker's goal is to establish probability, not certainty. Such discourse does not require the formal structures of scientific inquiry.

But that separation of the syllogism and the enthymeme does

---

3. Lloyd Bitzer, "The Rhetorical Situation," in *Philosophy and Rhetoric* 1 (Winter 1968): 15.

not mean that rhetoric is necessarily illogical or that it is never based on facts. As Grimaldi phrases it, Aristotle is simply acknowledging that there can be an epistemology of the *probable,* that human beings can use their intelligence to reason from less than complete and perfect knowledge about the real world and still arrive at rational and useful conclusions.[4]

Rhetors cannot expect to move people to action or to conviction in an uncertain world by appealing only to their intelligence. Speakers who hope to persuade or even to teach effectively must work with the whole personalities of their listeners, actively engaging their wills and their emotions and showing them that they share common interests and common goals with the speaker. And Aristotle believes that the best way to engage the audience's complete attention and establish common ground with it is by using the enthymeme. Basing an argument on an enthymeme necessarily involves drawing the audience's attitudes, beliefs, and experience into the structure of the argument. Those attitudes, beliefs, and experience form the groundwork for the argument; the very fact that the rhetor does not need to articulate them establishes a bond of intimacy and trust between speaker and listener. That bond enhances the speaker's ethical appeal and predisposes the listener to yield to the persuasion. So an enthymeme really represents a *process,* a dynamic activity—the listener or reader contributes to his own persuasion.

Let's take an example. Suppose one wants to argue that in the long run we really do not have much to fear from Russia because its scientists are not able to engage in the kind of free intellectual inquiry that is necessary if a country is going to compete successfully in this age of high technology. (John Stuart Mill makes a similar kind of argument at the conclusion of *On Liberty.*) The enthymeme that underlies this argument is this: Any country that keeps its scientists from engaging in free intellectual inquiry cannot compete in an age of high technology, so we do not have much to fear from Russia. If most people who understand formal de-

4. William M. A. Grimaldi, *Studies in the Philosophy of Aristotle's Rhetoric* (Wiesbaden: Franz Steiner Verlag GmbH, 1972), p. 16.

ductive reasoning were asked to furnish the missing premise in this argument, they would probably say it is this: Russia is a country that prohibits its scientists from engaging in free intellectual inquiry.

But this enthymeme represents much more that an abbreviated syllogism and contains many more assumptions than that contained in the missing premise. Simply supplying that premise does not lay out the argument for objective analysis, for concealed beneath the surface is a rich lode of other significant assumptions. First, the speaker has assumed that she has a western audience who brings an anti-Soviet bias to the argument and probably wants to believe Russia cannot triumph. The speaker also assumes that the audience brings a pro-technology bias to the argument and that it believes that high technological achievements make a nation superior. The implication that she shares these assumptions enhances her stature with the audience, reassures them about their own attitudes, and makes them receptive to her argument. She also appeals to the audience's emotions with terms like "free intellectual inquiry" and "compete successfully" since those phrases are what Richard Weaver calls "god terms" in our culture. And she invites the audience to supply from its own knowledge the premise that Russia prohibits its scientists from engaging in free intellectual inquiry; her listeners can supply their own supporting examples from what they have read about Andrei Sakharov and others.

The fact that the listeners already have such examples in mind and do not have to be told of them enlarges the part they themselves play in the persuasion. In developing her argument, the speaker would probably go on to expand on her thesis, furnishing examples that would be less familiar to the audience, and mentioning technological breakthroughs that have come from laboratories in which only pure research was being done, believing that the audience would respond to such support.

Anyone skilled in analyzing persuasion could dig even deeper into this hypothetical argument, but I think I have made my point sufficiently. What one must understand about this kind of argument, however, is that it cannot be developed out of context or by formula. The person arguing cannot set up the argument before knowing the audience because it holds the key to the appropriate strategy. Thus the rhetor must quickly and accurately assess what the audience brings to the occasion and choose examples that will suit that particular audience, given its preknowledge and predisposition. The enthymeme itself thus becomes an investigative tool, a stimulus to discovery, and an aid to finding rhetorical support. Aristotle devotes much of the *Rhetoric* to suggesting guidelines for analyzing audience and to an explanation of the *topoi* or places that one can look for supporting examples that suit the specific situation.

Both McBurney and Grimaldi believe that Aristotle spends so much time on that advice, not because he believes that rhetoric is necessarily manipulative in the pejorative sense, but because, as he says early in the *Rhetoric*, it is the rhetorician's task to discover in any subject the elements of that subject that can be used to persuade another; then that person can use his or her own free will to judge the worth of the argument. He is only affirming a principle on which almost all modern rhetoricians agree: that all discourse occurs within a cultural context in which the knowledge and attitudes of the parties involved necessarily qualify the statements that are made. That principle is the heart of the enthymeme.

Now if this view of Aristotle's *Rhetoric* is a reasonable one— and more recent scholars such as Lloyd Bitzer and John Gage give it convincing support—what has gone wrong? Why have centuries of scholars in both the sciences and the humanities so misunderstood the enthymeme in particular and rhetoric in general?

The Split between Speculative and Practical Intellect

I think we can begin to understand the frame of mind that has led to the neglect of rhetoric and the enthymeme and the kind of situational and pragmatic thinking it embodies if we consider the polarized attitudes that began to develop among intellectuals more than two thousand years ago. Scholars working in philosophy and science have traditionally taken the view that discourse in their disciplines should be objective and impersonal and should deal with universals. In contrast, they thought of the discourse of rhetoricians as emotional, personal, and dealing with particulars. (Neither view is really accurate, of course.) But the most important difference, and the one I think has most radically affected the scientists' and philosophers' view of rhetoric, is the domain into which each kind of discourse has been placed. As Grimaldi points out, those who engage in scientific and philosophical discourse and use the tools of deduction, induction, and dialectic have been presumed to be exercising the *speculative intellect*. Those who engage in persuasive discourse and use the rhetorical tools of the enthymeme and examples taken from experience or human observation have been presumed to be using the *practical intellect.*[5]

In the introductory chapter of his text *The New Rhetoric,* Chaim Perelman makes virtually the same point in different terms. He refers to "that age-old debate between those who stand for the truth and those who stand for opinion, between philosophers seeking the absolute and rhetors involved in action."[6] He then defines the terms he will use in his book by making this distinction: "We are going to apply the term *persuasive* to argumentation that only claims validity for a particular audience, and the term *convincing* to argumentation that presumes to gain the adherence of every rational being."[7] I think this distinction that philosophers have historically insisted upon explains, at least partially, why the enthymeme has fallen out of favor with scholars and the decline of rhetoric in English departments.

In its pure form, each category of intellect is presumed to engage

5. Grimaldi, p. 25.
6. Chaim Perelman and L. Olbrechts-Tyteca, *The New Rhetoric: A Treatise on Argumentation,* trans. by John Wilkinson and Purcell Weaver (Notre Dame and London: University of Notre Dame Press, 1969), p. 26.
7. Ibid., p. 28.

in a very different kind of activity. Those who use speculative intellect are searching for absolutes, for truth with a capital T, ultimate reality in the Platonic sense. They are engaged in scientific discourse or philosophical dialectic, concerned with natural laws and first principles. They work apart from the everyday world, and *logos* dominates their discourse; *ethos* and *pathos* play almost no part in their demonstrations and dialectic.

Those who use practical intellect, on the other hand, focus on the realm of human activity, the world of the contingent, the uncertain, and the changeable. They are engaged in argument and debate, in solving immediate problems and formulating workable policies. They are using rhetoric, and, as Grimaldi points out, "Rhetoric incorporated as integral components *logos, ethos,* and *pathos* and addressed itself to the whole man."[8]

Aristotle, of course, was one of the great speculative intellects of his time, an impressive scientist and dialectician. But he had also a great practical intellect and saw no necessary split between the two faculties. For him, it was as important for a man to be skilled in rhetoric as to be skilled in the art of scientific inquiry, and it was as natural for him to turn his attention to the arts of rhetoric as it was to focus on aesthetics or ethics or analytics. In fact, Grimaldi argues that the *Rhetoric* is an integral part of Aristotle's total body of work and quite consistent with his other treatises. In his view, Aristotle did not think rhetoric was inferior to dialectical or scientific reasoning, only different, and he vigorously rejects criticisms, such as that of W. D. Ross, that the *Rhetoric* is "a curious jumble of literary criticism with second-rate logic, ethics, politics, and jurisprudence, mixed by the cunning of one who knows well how the weaknesses of the human heart are to be played on."[9]

Unfortunately, more professors seem to have agreed with Ross than with Grimaldi, and consequently rhetoric, and with it the art

8. Grimaldi, pp. 16–17.
9. Ibid., p. 55.

of the enthymeme, has fallen on hard times in many circles. I want to speculate briefly on some of those reasons, both historic and contemporary.

Historically, I think, the dislike for and condescension to the domain of the practical intellect runs deep in the academic temperament. Plato's quest for the absolute truth is more attractive to the contemplative nature of the scholar than Aristotle's quest for human happiness and justice. Consequently, many intellectuals have cut themselves off from the material world in the name of pure research, saying that the true scholar or scientist doesn't worry about practical considerations or worldly concerns. They contend that to appeal to what Perelman calls a "particular audience" would corrupt their work by causing them to compromise. Only what Perelman calls the "universal audience" of fully rational persons deserves their attention. If that audience actually contains only a few people, that doesn't matter because they are working on a plane that only a few exceptional souls are capable of understanding. They disdain the practical intellect and all activity connected with it.

Now this is profoundly Platonic, of course, but the consequences of such attitudes can reach far beyond the realm of metaphysical speculation. In his book *The Sleepwalkers,* a biographical study of the great astronomers, Arthur Koestler claims that the influence of Plato and his disciples halted scientific progress in the Western world for two thousand years. Plato's "pure" vision that told him that the solar system must be arranged in a perfect sphere and all motion of the planets set at a uniform speed effectively stopped further investigation into astronomy until the time of Kepler.[10]

To this kind of Platonic temperament, rhetoric is anathema because it necessarily means becoming involved in all those areas of life that the reclusive mind, which would rather grapple with the abstract than the concrete, despises and fears. And one can see how people of this intellectual bent would particularly despise the

10. Arthur Koestler, *The Sleepwalkers* (New York: The Universal Library, Grosset and Dunlap, 1959), p. 57.

enthymeme as embodying the worst in rhetoric. They would view it as a corruption of the syllogism, a fraudulent form of logic. That bias comes through when one hears the enthymeme defined as "an invalid syllogism" or "an incomplete syllogism." By using those definitions they imply that people who use enthymemes are either such sloppy thinkers that they do not recognize their supposed premises or that they are suppressing premises in an attempt to mislead their audience.

As James Kinneavy's article in *The Rhetorical Tradition and Modern Writing* points out, this attitude toward rhetoric is a deeply antihumanistic view, and one that has profoundly affected the teaching of writing in our English departments and in universities as a whole. It has displaced rhetoric from its historical role as the center of liberal education and split composition teaching from its roots in the humanistic tradition.[11]

The Current Neglect of the Enthymeme

But now that rhetoric is reclaiming its place in the humanities and we see a resurgence of the classical traditions, why does the enthymeme continue to be neglected by most composition theorists, who obviously are not scholarly elitists? If they were, they wouldn't have chosen to specialize in anything as practical and worldly as teaching writing. Certainly they recognize and respect the basic principles of classical rhetorical theory—witness the emphasis on audience and purpose and the dynamic relationship of writer and reader—but they ignore the enthymeme even though it occupies such a central position in Aristotle's *Rhetoric*. Why?

There is no simple answer, of course. Styles change in both teaching and research and not always for well thought out reasons. But I believe that we can find one plausible explanation if we look at the divisions that have emerged in the discipline of modern rhetoric in recent years.

11. James L. Kinneavy, "Restoring the Humanities: The Return of Rhetoric from Exile," in *The Rhetorical Tradition and Modern Writing*, ed. James J. Murphy (New York: Modern Language Association, 1982), pp. 20–21.

In a recent book titled *Assessing Writers' Knowledge and Composing Processes,* my colleague Lester Faigley and three of his associates in a large research project have identified and defined three current schools of thought on the composing process.[12] The first they call the literary view of composing. Not surprisingly, this view of composing has dominated English departments for the approximately one hundred years that they have existed in this country. It has been particularly strong since 1914, when faculty professing the discipline of speech and rhetoric split off from English departments, leaving the teaching of writing to literature professors and graduate students in literature departments.

Richard Young calls this literary view of composition teaching "romantic" since it reflects the theories of composing held by nineteenth-century romantics who held that writing is a nonrational activity that cannot really be taught because the creative process cannot be analyzed or prescribed. Faigley suggests that roots of this belief go back to Plato and his distrust of rational processes of inquiry for seeking the truth.

It is hardly surprising to find that most professors who consider themselves primarily literary scholars still cling to this view. First, it allows them to focus on written products, which have been the center of their professional training, rather than on the writing process, which they believe is mysterious and inaccessible. Second, it frees them of the awesome responsibility for teaching writing, since if no one understands how people write, it must follow that no one can know how to teach students to write. Naturally, teachers who hold these views are not going to rely on either logic or rhetoric in their writing classes. And it is still true that most of the writing teachers in this country come from this romantic tradition.

It does seem surprising, however, that people who consider themselves specialists in the teaching of writing should hold simi-

---

12. Lester Faigley et al., *Assessing Writers' Knowledge and Composing Processes* (Norwood, N.J.: Ablex Press, 1985).

lar views. Yet as James Berlin and others have pointed out, the
teaching philosophies of several well-known and influential contemporary writing theorists fall into this romantic category. Gordon Rohman and James Moffett advocate meditation as a way for
the writer to get in touch with the subconscious in order to start
writing. Donald Murray speaks of the two selves writing; one
creating spontaneously and nonrationally, the other simultaneously acting as monitor and editor.[13] Peter Elbow (*Writing Without
Teachers*), Ken McCrorie (*Uptaught*), William Coles (*The Personal I*), and Barrett Mandel are other prominent names in this group
of teachers who promote an "expressionist" approach to teaching,
and who feel that the principal job of a writing teacher is to help
the student writer get in touch with his or her subconscious or
authentic self and then write honestly from that self. For such
teachers, syllogisms and enthymemes will play no part in this
process.

Now I am not denigrating these particular individuals nor the
expressionist approach to composition; I have learned from all of
them—especially Donald Murray. They have contributed a great
deal to the profession and have provided a healthy counterforce
to composition textbooks that rely on formulas and suggest that
the writing process consists of arranging already known content
according to conventional models. But I think we must certainly
acknowledge the influence of these expressionist teachers in trying
to understand some of the reasons why comparatively few teachers seem to be interested in teaching the strategies of classical
rhetoric in their composition courses. Their books are well known
and popular; they have published extensively in the professional
journals, and I know that all of them draw large and enthusiastic
audiences when they speak. In all these forums they stress that we
should not depend on formulas or formal patterns in our composition classrooms. And if writing teachers perceive the enthy-

13. Donald Murray, "Teaching the Other Self: The Writer's First Reader," in
College Composition and Communication 33 (May 1982): 140–147.

meme as a kind of formula for structuring thought—and frequently they do—then those who belong to the Elbow/McCrorie/Coles school of composition will reject it.

Another and probably equally influential school views composing as a cognitive task, similar to problem solving. Those who hold this view believe that "the goal of composing is to communicate, that writing abilities follow a developmental sequence, that composing is an orderly process from which general principles can be abstracted, and that these general principles can be used to teach writing."[14] The theories of Linda Flower and John Hayes that have been developed in research at Carnegie-Mellon University underlie this view of composing, but, as Faigley and his co-authors point out, much of it is based on assumptions that derive from Aristotle. His suggestions for assessing one's audience and seeking the appropriate means by which to appeal to it correspond closely to Flower's and Hayes's suggestions for evaluating the rhetorical situation, setting goals and subgoals, and searching the long-term memory for material to develop those goals. But to my knowledge, neither Flower and Hayes nor any of the composition theorists who advocate the cognitive approach to composing ever suggest using the enthymeme as a specific invention strategy. Rather they describe a writer's invention process as a series of individualized, top-down problem-solving steps that do not depend on any system or external guidelines. A writer working under their scheme might well use a rhetorical syllogism, but he or she would not consciously employ it as a device for generating either content or organization.

The third approach identified by Faigley and his coauthors is the social view of composing, which sees the writer at the center of a discourse community and holds that the composing process is largely determined by the demands of that community. Those who profess this view have not constructed any composing theories to correspond to their beliefs. I think Aristotle would feel quite comfortable with this school of composing, and its adher-

14. Faigley et al.

ents may soon call upon his principles to support their theories. When they do the enthymeme may reappear in the professional forum of journals and conferences and in the textbooks that reflect the current teaching paradigms.

Returning the Enthymeme to the Composition Classroom

Such a reappearance of the enthymeme would be a healthy development, I think, because used imaginatively the enthymeme has the power to generate content and suggest patterns of organization in almost any writing situation.

First, we can show students how to define the enthymeme that underlies their arguments and then teach them how to identify the common ground they are assuming exists between them and their audience and to think about what information that audience has that they can draw on for examples and support. As Professor John Gage of the University of Oregon says in an article in *Rhetoric Review,* spelling out the central enthymeme of an argument doesn't necessarily solve the problems of composing that argument, but it does bring them into view and help the writer to begin to discover specific elements that can be used to persuade the audience. Then the writer can look for places to find those elements.[15] An article by Lawrence Green on using the enthymeme in writing classes also points out that having students define and articulate the syllogism that underlies an argument helps them to see whether their basic premises are value statements, normative statements, or cause and effect statements. They can then judge whether they are going to be able to build a plausible argument from their premises.[16]

Second, I think we can use the enthymeme to introduce students to the critical concept of the "rhetorical situation"; that is,

15. John Gage, "Teaching the Enthymeme: Invention and Arrangement," in *Rhetoric Review* 2 (September 1983): 38–50.
16. Lawrence D. Green, "Enthymemic Invention and Structural Prediction," in *College English* 41 (February 1980): 623–634.

the realization that writing is always a dynamic activity that involves the writer, the audience, and a purpose or an occasion, and that every part of the situation necessarily affects every other part. I believe that this concept must form the foundation of any modern writing course. But, as anyone who has taught novice writers knows, it is an extremely difficult one to teach. I have decided that my students face their problems with audience in the same way that alcoholics face their drinking problems; they deny the problem exists. Yet as we know, perhaps the most crucial difference between skilled and unskilled writers is that skilled writers almost invariably respond to the whole rhetorical situation when they write, and unskilled writers respond only to the topic. So one of our most important tasks with beginning writers is to show them how to analyze the components of their rhetorical situation and help them understand how those components control their writing processes. When earlier I analyzed the audience and rhetor in the argument about Russian scientists, I tried to demonstrate how those components can be dramatized. Having students work together in groups to write in-class analyses of such rhetorical situations can help them develop the habit of analyzing in such a manner for their own papers.

For example, ask students to create a scenario that would help them develop the paper based on science departments discriminating against women. One could do it like this: Imagine that you are a well-known woman physicist at a major state university and your department has asked you to write an article for the departmental bulletin for junior and senior honors students. At least half of those students are women, and you're concerned that they may not know what to expect if they choose to go on to graduate work in physics. Though you don't want to discourage these young women, you definitely want to give them realistic advice about the problems women scientists have frequently faced, and then let them make their own decisions. Assume the young women to whom you are writing are optimistic high achievers who have never encountered any sex discrimination as undergraduates, and think it's something that doesn't happen any more. Thus this group is not going to be a particularly receptive audience.

Once a writer has created this kind of script, it becomes an invention strategy. She can then decide what common knowledge she and her readers have—such as the information that in every science department in the university, men faculty far outnumber women faculty and that men hold all the administrative positions. They also share the information that nearly all science textbooks arc written by men, etc. After that, she can decide what kind of examples of sex discrimination she will need as new information—salary comparisons, promotions, distribution of grants, specific cases of discrimination, etc. Then she can decide if she has enough material to make her case and how to organize that material. Finally, she must think about what important assumptions she and the women students share—for instance, that women are as bright and capable as men, that women are entitled to equal pay and promotion with men, and that university departments have a moral obligation to treat their women faculty fairly. The shared assumptions will control the tone of the writing.

Teachers can also point out how differently students would have to structure the argument if they postulate a different audience and purpose. For instance, have them imagine a case in which the writer was an angry junior professor writing to the U.S. Equal Opportunity Office to complain about sex discrimination in her department. Now the argument changes in important ways because she and the audience do not share much information and she will have to provide much more than the first writer. Nor do she and her audience necessarily share many assumptions about a department's moral obligations. This time the shared premises will be about legal issues. The style of this writing will also differ because the complaint will be more formal and objective.

Students will do this kind of script writing reluctantly at first, but gradually most of them will warm to it. Eventually they realize that it really does make their writing tasks easier.

Moreover, I don't think one has to teach formal patterns of

logic and reasoning in order to show students how to use enthymemes effectively. The danger is that if we get into formal deductive logic and teach the enthymeme as part of that process, we risk
suggesting that the enthymeme has no legitimate status of its own.
Rather we imply that the way to judge the value of the enthymeme is to expand it into a syllogism by showing its missing
premise and then assess its validity. I have been guilty of doing
just that. But most of the time the person who argues from an
enthymeme is not trying to *prove* a proposition; he or she is only
trying to establish high probability. It we try to refute such an
argument by calling it logically invalid, we are missing the point.
If an audience finds the argument I made earlier about women
scientists being discriminated against in male-dominated departments a persuasive one, it does so because it is sensitive to such
problems, because it believes in professional equality, and because it can draw on its own knowledge and experience for supporting examples. It will accept the argument even though it cannot
be *proved* with an airtight syllogism. One cannot negate the pragmatic conclusions expressed by an enthymeme simply by introducing a few exceptions to the rule.

The enthymeme also works well in the context of two other
kinds of informal reasoning that are mentioned in many of today's
rhetoric texts: Rogerian argument and Toulmin logic. In Rogerian
or nonthreatening argument, a writer can make good use of the
enthymeme to discover what premises he or she shares with the
audience and what common ground exists that can form the basis
for communication and change.[17] The writer who uses Toulmin
logic, the legalistically-oriented method that focuses on ways to
establish probability through a system of claims and warrants, can
also make good use of enthymemes. By phrasing the proposition
that he or she wants to prove in the abbreviated form of an
enthymeme, a writer can quickly determine how the claim and

warrant are related and what kind of backing for the claim the audience is likely to require.[18]

Using the ideas I have mentioned here and others from the articles by Gage and by Green, perhaps teachers will find that Aristotle's enthymeme, misunderstood and neglected for so long in composition classes but kept alive in speech communication, can once again begin to serve important functions in the composition classroom. The enthymene can be used as a powerful tool for discovery and as a method for introducing students to the patterns of argument and rational thought. But I think its greatest power is still that which Aristotle attributed to it in the first place: the power to probe the rhetorical situation and discover the available means of persuasion for a particular case and for a particular audience. For rhetoric is always pragmatic and so is the enthymeme. As pragmatists ourselves, we should learn once more to use it.

18. Toulmin logic is described at length and adapted to the needs of advanced composition students in my *Successful Writing* (New York: W. W. Norton and Co., 1981), pp. 65–70.

James L. Kinneavy

5 *Kairos*: A Neglected Concept in Classical Rhetoric

History of Kairos and Contemporary Parallels

This volume of essays is an attempt to show the relevance of some important concepts of classical rhetoric to modern composition. Anyone in the field of rhetoric has undoubtedly already encountered the concepts being discussed by the other contributors; practical reasoning, *topoi,* enthymeme, *aitia,* and *telos* hardly need justification in such a symposium. But *kairos* is not listed in Lanham's *A Handlist of Rhetorical Terms,*[1] nor in the four volumes of the *Dictionary of the History of Ideas,*[2] nor in the two

1. Richard A. Lanham, *A Handlist of Rhetorical Terms: A Guide for Students of English Literature* (Berkeley, Calif.: University of California Press, 1969). *Kairos* is mentioned in Heinrich Lausberg, *Handbuch der literarischen Rhetorik: Eine Grundlegung der Literaturwissenschaft* (Munich: Max Heuber Verlag, 1960), but not in Henri Morier, *Dictionnaire de poétique et de rhétorique* (Paris: Presses Universitaires de France, 1961).

2. Philip P. Wiener, ed., *Dictionary of the History of Ideas: Studies of Selected Pivotal Ideas* (New York: Scribner's, 1973).

volumes of *The Great Ideas: A Syntopicon,*[3] which accompanies the Great Books of the Western World series. Yet a strong case can be made for the thesis that *kairos* is the dominating concept in sophistic, Platonic, and, in a sense, even in Ciceronian rhetoric. This essay is an attempt to reassert its importance for a contemporary theory of composition.

The second part of the essay will be an extended definition of *kairos,* but provisionally it might be defined as the right or opportune time to do something, or right measure in doing something. Often the two notions are joined; thus, the righteous anger justified in a war situation would be excessive and improper in a family dispute: the *kairos* would not be right. Before expanding and clarifying this definition, it might be worthwhile to give a brief sketch of the history of the notion and an explanation for its neglect by many rhetoricians, both historical and contemporary.

Although the word does not occur in Homer, it already occurs in Hesiod (seventh century B.C.), whose statement "Observe due measure, and proportion [*kairos*] is best in all things"[4] became a proverb. It is a critical concept in the poetry of Pindar (fl. fifth century B.C.), where the meaning of due or proper measure is given more emphasis than it had been in either Hesiod or Theognis.[5] The notion of *kairos* was embodied in several of the maxims attributed to the Seven Sages of Greece, particularly "Nothing in excess" and "Seal your word with silence and your silence with the right time," both of which were sometimes specifically linked with Solon.[6] It seems clear that with the influence of Hesiod,

3. Mortimer J. Adler, ed., *The Great Ideas: A Syntopicon of Great Books of the Western World,* No. 2 of *Great Books of the Western World,* ed. Ribert Maynard Hutchins (Chicago, Ill.: Encyclopaedia Britannica, Inc., 1951). *Kairos* is not even mentioned in the large article on "Time," nor in the bibliographic references.
4. Henry George Liddell and Robert Scott, comps., *A Greek-English Lexicon,* revised by Sir Henry Stuart Jones and Robert McKenzie (Oxford: At the Clarendon Press, 1968), p. 859.
5. Doro Levi, "Il *Kairos* Attraverso la Letteratura Greca," *Rendiconti della Reale Accademia Nazionale dei Lincei. Classe di scienzia Morali,* RV, vol. 32 (1923), pp. 266 [260–281]. Henceforth referred to as "*Kairos.*"
6. Ibid., p. 274.

Pindar, and some of the sayings of the Seven Sages, the concept of *kairos* had become a part of the educational ideals of early Greece. As Levi says, "To the Socratic 'Know thyself,' the pre-Socratic ethic juxtaposed its own 'Know the opportunity,' *kairon gnothi.*"[7]

The pre-Socratic prominence of *kairos* in Greek thought can particularly be seen in the Pythagorean school. Rostagni has analyzed this aspect of Pythagorean thought more than anyone else. He states that to Pythagoreans this maxim was inscribed, "The most important thing in every action is *kairos.*"[8] Untersteiner states this in another way: for the Pythagoreans, *kairos* was "one of the laws of the universe."[9] Pythagoras and his school gave further complexity to the concept of *kairos,* linking it closely with the basis of all virtue, particularly justice, and consequently with civic education. Indeed, several of the Pythagoreans made the mastery of *kairos* to be the essence of philosophy.[10] Others considered it a faculty on a par with the soul and the intellect.[11]

The sophists Prodicus, Antiphon, Hippias, and probably also Protagoras used the concept of *kairos* in their philosophical and rhetorical systems. But, as Untersteiner has thoroughly demonstrated, it was Gorgias who made *kairos* the cornerstone of his entire epistemology, ethics, aesthetics, and rhetoric. Gorgias and some of the other sophists carried the implications of the relativism of different situations to such lengths that Plato countered with the stability and permanence of his world of ideas. Yet even Plato did not dispense with *kairos,* particularly in rhetoric. And Plato also used *kairos* as the foundation on which to construct his

7. Ibid., p. 275.
8. Augusto Rostagni, "Un Nuovo Capitolo nella Storia della Retorica e della Sofistica," *Studi Italiani di filologia classica,* N.S., vol. 2, 1–2 (1922), p. 165 [148–201]. He finds this statement in Iamblichus, *Life of Pythagoras,* p. 49. I am using an unpublished translation of Rostagni's article by Philip Sipiora, p. 29.
9. Mario Untersteiner, *The Sophists,* trans. Kathleen Freeman (Oxford: Basil Blackwell, 1954), p. 110.
10. Ibid., p. 82.
11. Levi, *"Kairos,"* p. 275.

theory of virtue as a mean between two extremes, the theory developed still further by Aristotle.

With Gorgias and Plato, the concept of *kairos* undoubtedly reached its apogee. Aristotle, interested more in the art of rhetoric than in the act of rhetoric, gave *kairos* considerably less prominence than did Plato. Among Hellenistic thinkers, the concept was not nearly so important as it had been in Hellenic times, although some Stoic philosophers used the notion in discussing the ethics of suicide, cannibalism, and other actions under certain circumstances.[12]

But in Stoicism, particularly Latin Stoicism, the concept of *kairos* merged with that of *prepon* (propriety or fitness), as Max Pohlenz has shown in his admirable study of this latter concept.[13] In this guise, *kairos* is the dominating concept in both Cicero's ethics and his rhetoric. Consequently, it is not inaccurate to say that *kairos,* with the related concept of *prepon,* was a major influence in much of classical rhetoric in antiquity, particularly with the Pythagoreans, the sophists, Plato, and Cicero.

However, although the Ciceronian notion of propriety persisted throughout the medieval and Renaissance periods, the residual influence of *kairos* is almost a negligible chapter in the history of rhetoric since antiquity, partly because of the overwhelming influence of Aristotelian rhetoric in this history. This partially explains the absence of *kairos* in the dictionaries and handbooks of rhetoric that I alluded to earlier.

Three Italian scholars in this century are mainly responsible for the recognition that *kairos* played such an important role in Greek rhetoric and thought generally. In 1922 Augusto Rostagni wrote a monograph-size article entitled (in English) "A New Chapter in Rhetoric and Sophistry."[14] He carefully traced the history of the

---

12. A. A. Long, *Hellenistic Philosophy: Stoics, Epicureans, Sceptics* (London: Gerald Duckworth and Co., Ltd., 1974), p. 206.

13. Max Pohlenz, *"To Prepon:* Ein Beitrag zur Geschichte des griechischen Geistes," *Nachrichten von der Gesellschaft der Wissenschaften zu Goettingen, Philologisch-historische Klasse, Heft 1* (1933), pp. 54–55 [53–92]. Reprinted, *Kleine Schriften,* ed. Heinrich Dorrie (Hildesheim: G. Olms, 1965), vol. 2, pp. 100–139.

14. Rostagni, see note 8.

notion and particularly demonstrated the dominating influence of the Pythagorean school, especially on Gorgias and Plato. In the next two years Doro Levi published two additonal articles on *kairos*, one specifically on the importance of the concept in Plato's philosophy.[15] In 1948 Mario Untersteiner published his innovative and controversial study, *The Sophists*, in which he analyzed in great detail the influence of *kairos* in sophistic thought, especially in that of Gorgias. The final voice that has called the attention of the twentieth century to *kairos* has been that of the German theologian Paul Tillich, who made the concept of *kairos*, as it is presented in the New Testament, one of the foundation ideas of his entire theology. His works include at least five major statements on *kairos*.[16] Although Tillich does not address the issue of *kairos* from a rhetorician's point of view, his ideas, I will attempt to show, can be applied to the matter of teaching composition.

These major scholars have been calling our attention to *kairos* for more than sixty years, but few rhetoricians have given them much attention. Yet I am firmly convinced that rhetoric desperately needs the notion of *kairos*. I have made several pleas for its reincorporation into the systematic study of composition because I see it as a dominant motif in disciplines related to our own. The concept of situational context, which is a modern term for *kairos*, is in the forefront of research and thought in many areas.[17] The phrase "rhetorical situation" has almost become a slogan in the

15. Levi, see note 5 for the general article; "Il Concetto di *Kairos* e la Filosofia di Platone," *Accademia Nazionale dei Lincei, Roma. Classe di Scienze Morali, Storiche, Critiche e Filologiche*, Rendiconti vol. 33 (1924), pp. 93–118. Henceforth referred to as "Concetto."

16. See Paul Tillich, "Kairos and Logos," in *The Interpretation of History*, trans. N. A. Rasetzki and Elsa Talmey (New York: Scribner's, 1936). Henceforth referred to as "Kairos." See Also "Kairos and Kairoi," *Systematic Theology* (Chicago, Ill.: The University of Chicago Press, 1963), vol. 2, pp. 369–372; "Kairos I," *Der Widerstreit von Raum und Zeit: Schriften zur Geschichtsphilosophie, Gesammelte Werke*, VI, pp. 10–28; "Kairos II, Ideen zur Geisteslage der Gegenwart," VI, pp. 29–41; and "Kairos und Utopie," VI, pp. 149–165.

17. James L. Kinneavy, "The Relation of the Whole to the Part in Interpretation Theory and in the Composing Process," in *Linguistics, Stylistics, and the Teaching of Composition*, ed. Donald McQuade (Akron, Ohio: Language and Style, 1979), pp. 1–23. Henceforth referred to as "Relation."

field of speech communications since Lloyd Bitzer's article on the subject appeared in 1964.[18] I have argued that the relevance of the immediate situation is at the heart of Freudian dream analysis; that Kenneth Burke's pentad is an attempt to erect the major dimensions of a situation; that the "emic," as opposed to the "etic," approach of the tagmemic linguistics of Kenneth Pike has a similar emphasis; that the ethnomethodology approach in modern anthropology is a movement in exactly the same direction; that the hermeneutic forestructure of Heidegger, the prejudices of Gadamer, and the demythologizing movement of Bultmann are evidences of the same insistence on situational and cultural context in philosophy and theology; that the strong critical reaction against the near autonomy of the text in literary criticism has resulted in different emphases on the individuality of the reader's response in such different writers as Jacques Derrida, Edward Said, Stanley Fish, and Josue Harari; and that the current theories in pragmatics, of Bobrow and Norman, of Minsky, and of Schank all stress the importance of the unique background of the interpreter to the business of interpreting anything.[19] Even in composition theory itself, the necessity of a cultural and informational background has been stressed by E. D. Hirsch.[20]

All of these voices saying ultimately the same thing ought to convince us that some consideration in any rhetorical theory must be given to the issue raised by the concept of *kairos*—the appropriateness of the discourse to the particular circumstances of the time, place, speaker, and audience involved.

If this is so, it may be that modern treatments of situational context can learn something from the handling of the same topic

18. Lloyd F. Bitzer, "The Rhetorical Situation," *Philosophy and Rhetoric* 1 (1968): 1–14.

19. On Freudian dream analysis, see Kinneavy, "Relation," p. 17; and p. 22, note 80, for many references. My other arguments are developed in James L. Kinneavy, "Contemporary Rhetoric," in *The Present State of Scholarship in Historical and Contemporary Rhetoric,* ed. Winifred Bryan Horner (Columbia, Mo.: University of Missouri Press, 1983), pp. 174–177 [167–213].

20. E. D. Hirsch, Jr., "Culture and Literacy," *Journal of Basic Writing* 3 (Fall/Winter 1980): 27–47.

in antiquity. I would argue that they can, particularly in the ethical and educational realms. Consequently, it may be worthwhile to analyze the notion of *kairos* in an attempt to isolate its various components in the hope that the concept of *kairos* can contribute something of value to modern composition theory.

The Complex Concept of Kairos in Greek Rhetoric

This brief historical survey has already suggested that *kairos* is a complex concept, not easily reduced to a simple formula. I would like to analyze the various factors of the concept, considering in sequence the two fundamental elements embodied in five major areas in which the concept was relevant. In the analysis, I am following the findings of Rostagni, Levi, Untersteiner, and Tillich, although I have some qualifications about the last three, qualifications that will become clear in the sequel.

The Basic Concept: Two Components

The two basic elements of the concept are already seen in Hesiod and continue unabated through Cicero. They are the principle of right timing and the principle of a proper measure. Usually they are joined in a single concept, although individual occurrences of the term may focus on one or the other aspect. In the sense of "right" time, *kairos* may be opposed to the more routine *chronos,* although this opposition is not consistent in Hellenic, Hellenistic, and New Testament Greek.[21] Sometimes *kairos* can be viewed as neutral and a "good time" (*eukairos*), as opposed to a time without *kairos* (*akairos*).[22]

The second element is more elusive. The propriety of the concept of *kairos* is sometimes quite explicit, as in the proverb derived from Hesiod, "Observe good measure, and proportion [*kairos*] is

---

21. See James Barr, *Biblical Words for Time,* 2nd ed. (London: S.C.M. Press, 1969), pp. 20–21.
22. See Plato, *Phaedrus,* trans and intro. by W. C. Helmbold and W. G. Rabinowitz (Indianapolis, Ind.: The Bobbs-Merrill Co., Inc., 1958), pp. 272a.

best in all things," but other times it is only implicit. An example of this is the *locus classicus* of the rhetorical use of the notion of *kairos* in Plato. This occurs in the *Phaedrus* after Socrates has carefully constructed all of the basic dimensions of an ideal rhetoric. He summarizes his conclusions and then adds another dimension:

Since it is in fact the function of speech to influence souls, a man who is going to be a speaker must know how many kinds of souls there are. Let us, then, state that they are of this or that sort, so that individuals also will be of this or that type. Again, the distinctions that apply here apply as well in the cases of speeches: they are of this or that number in type, and each type of one particular sort. So men of a special sort under the influence of speeches of a particular kind are readily persuaded to take action of a definite sort because of the qualitative correlation that obtains between speech and soul; while men of a different sort are hard to persuade because, in their case, this qualitative correlation does not obtain. Very well. When a student has attained an adequate grasp of these facts intellectually, he must next go on to see with his own eyes that they occur in the world of affairs and are operative in practice; he must acquire the capacity to confirm their existence through the sharp use of his senses. If he does not do this, no part of the theoretical knowledge he acquired as a student is as yet of any help to him. But it is only when he has the capacity to declare to himself with complete perception, in the presence of another, that here is the man and here the nature that was discussed theoretically at school—here, now present to him in actuality—to which he must apply *this* kind of speech in *this* sort of manner in order to obtain persuasion for *this* kind of activity—it is when he can do all this and when he has, in addition, grasped the concept of propriety of time [*kairos*]—when to speak and when to hold his tongue [*eukairos* and *akairos*], when to use brachylogy, piteous language, hyperbole for horrific effect, and, in a word, each of the specific devices of discourse he may have studied—it is only then, and not until then, that the finishing and perfecting touches will have been given to his science.[23]

In this passage Plato indicates the primacy of the notion of *kairos* to his rhetorical system. It is the capstone that gives meaning to the entire substructure of the art. The notion of propriety is only implicit, however, even though the translation uses the words "propriety of time" to translate *kairos*. Yet the translation

23. Ibid., pp. 271d–272b.

is quite accurate since the concept of propriety undergirds the entire passage. But the component of propriety and measure in rhetoric is much richer than just a sense of the adaptation of the speech to the audience. In order to read into the notion of *kairos* its full connotations, even in rhetoric, it is necessary to establish its rich dimensions. In addition to the rhetorical, they embrace ethical, educational, epistemological, and aesthetic levels, all of which are linked to each other.

The Ethical Dimension of Kairos

One of the most significant ethical components of *kairos* had to do with its close relation to justice, particularly in the Pythagoreans. Justice was defined as giving to each *according to merit,* that is, generously to those who had worked hard and parsimoniously to those who had shirked. Justice, therefore, was determined by circumstances: justice was *kairos.*[24] This combination was omnipresent in Pythagoras, according to Rostagni: "All of his [Pythagoras's] teachings, his influence as founder of a school and as expert and custodian of minds—everything is based on the combined principles of *kairos* and *dikaion* [justice]."[25]

This facet of *kairos* is obviously related to the proper measure aspect of *kairos,* which is linked with the word in its earliest historical occurrences in Hesiod, Theognis, and later, especially in Pindar. Gorgias, Antisthenes, and other sophists continued this ethical facet of *kairos,* although some of them also skirted dangerously with the extreme relativism that a notion of situational determinism could carry with it. Isocrates and others, for example, accuse Gorgias of carrying situational ethics to the point of complete relativism,[26] although Untersteiner and Rostagni dispute this accusation.[27]

---

24. Rostagni, p. 163.
25. Ibid., p. 168.
26. Untersteiner, pp. 198–199.
27. Ibid., pp. 155–156, 204.

Plato and Socrates were seriously concerned with the relativism implicit in such a situational ethic, and Plato's ethic is an attempt to provide an alternative. Yet, curiously, Plato's ethic is also grounded on the notion of *kairos*. Plato used the concept of proper measure and right time—the two fundamental components of the concept of *kairos*—to construct the doctrine of virtue as the mean between two extremes (excess and deficiency). This doctrine is further developed by Aristotle and emerges as the classic Greek doctrine of virtue.[28]

More than any one strand of *kairos*, this aspect is continued in the Latin concept of propriety, especially in Cicero. It is the basis of his entire ethical treatise on duties—according to one scholar, possibly the single most influential book, other than the Bible, in Western civilization.[29]

Any application of *kairos* to the teaching of composition can not ignore the ethical dimension of the notion.

The Epistemological Dimension of Kairos

A common epistemological thread is woven into the meaning of *kairos* from Pindar and Bacchylides, writing poetry in the fifth century B.C., through the Pythagoreans, Gorgias, and Plato, and is still found in the modern extrapolations of the concept made by Tillich, the twentieth-century theologian. At the risk of simplifying, let me provisionally say that *kairos* brings timeless ideas down into the human situations of historical time. It thus imposes value on the ideas and forces humans to make free decisions about these values. Let us flesh these ideas out with a little history.

Pindar and, to a lesser extent, Bacchylides felt that it was the task of the poet to make known the divine revelation to man. Pindar claims that his poems are from the gods, through the Muses.[30] Although the gods provide the message and the stim-

---

28. This argument for the *kairos* origin of the doctrine of the mean is drawn from Levi, "*Kairos*," pp. 277–279; see also Rostagni, p. 164.

29. A. E. Douglas, "Cicero the Philosopher," in *Cicero*, ed. T. P. Dorey (New York: Basic Books, Inc., 1965), p. 149.

30. C. M. Bowra, *Pindar* (Oxford: At the Clarendon Press, 1964), p. 5, cites

ulus to create, the poet must incorporate his god-given wisdom (*sophia*) in the work of his own crafting.[31] And Pindar felt that his contribution to the craft of poetry was his ability to single out the critical moment of a story (the *kairos*) and weave a short poem around it. He tells the story of Orestes in twenty-four lines, whereas his predecessor, Stesichorus, filled two books with the same story.[32] The divine ideas thus acquire a human value.[33]

Gorgias takes a more strident view of this process. The transcendent divine ideas take no account of the facts of human existence. To apply to man, the divine ideas must become immanent in human life through *kairos*. This can be achieved when the writer enters into the "psychological situation of whoever has perpetrated the deed [being written about], trying to understand its individual character."[34] This, for Gorgias, can come about only through the deceptions of persuasive rhetoric and poetry.[35]

It is very clear that in Plato's system, rhetorical thought becomes effective only at the moment of *kairos,* as the lengthy passage from the *Phaedrus* quoted above amply illustrates. And I have already called attention to the significance of the notion of *kairos* in Plato's ethic. In both rhetoric and ethic, Plato's world of ideas is brought down to earth by the notion of *kairos.*

Tillich has taken these Greek ideas and has drawn from them some theological, historical, and philosophical corollaries. Although I seriously disagree with some of his conclusions, his contrast of the two philsophical tendencies in Western thought, *kairos* and *logos,* is a valuable addition to the epistemological sketch here being attempted. Tillich distinguishes *logos* thinking as characterized by an emphasis on timelessness, on form, on law, on stasis, on method; he finds it the dominant pattern of Western

Olympia XI, line 10, Olympia IX, lines 100–104, and Olympia II, lines 86–88, to support this point.

31. Ibid., p. 21.
32. Gilbert Norwood, *Pindar* (Berkeley, Calif.: Univ. of California Press, 1945), pp. 168–172.
33. Untersteiner, p. 111.
34. Ibid., p. 104.
35. Ibid., pp. 108–114.

thought, from Plato and Aristotle through most of the Church Fathers, on to Descartes and Kant. Opposing this trend is *kairos* thinking, characterized by an emphasis on time, on change, on creation, on conflict, on fate, and on individuality. He cites Jakob Boehme, Duns Scotus, Luther, and the late Romantics as instances of this minority approach to Western thought.[36] He argues for the importance of the *kairos* approach because it brings theory into practice, it asserts the continuing necessity of free decision, it insists on the value and norm aspects of ideas, it champions a vital and concerned interest in knowledge because knowledge always is relevant to the situational context, and it provides a better solution to the problem of uniting idea and historical reality than the solution of either Hegel or Marx.[37] Tillich contends that Hegel sacrificed freedom by making historical reality follow the logical norms of ideality, and he maintains that Marx capitulated to relativism and sacrificed real knowledge by subordinating idea to historical situation.[38] He argues for the union of freedom and fate in *kairos* and for a less rigid notion of unchanging idea, a notion of a dynamic idea.[39]

One critic of Tillich argues that Tillich's concept of *kairos* is at least partially indebted to the Marxist concern for historical consciousness.[40] It certainly is closely allied to Walter Benjamin's notion of the importance of being aware of the "now-time," the revolutionary possibilities inherent in the moment, the "state of emergency" in which we live, the potentials for change inherent in the historical situation.[41]

36. Tillich, "Kairos," pp. 127–129.
37. Ibid., pp. 130–131, 134, 136–139, 143–148.
38. Ibid., pp. 152–157.
39. Ibid., pp. 157–164.
40. Raymond F. Bulman, "Theonomy and Technology," in *Kairos and Logos: Studies in the Roots and Implications of Tillich's Theology,* ed. John J. Carey (Cambridge, Mass.: North American Paul Tillich Society, 1978), p. 240.
41. Walter Benjamin, *Illuminations,* trans. Harry Zoln, ed. Hannah Arendt (New York: Schocken Books, 1969), pp. 257–262.

The Rhetorical Dimension of Kairos

I already established the rhetorical dimension of *kairos* in Platonic rhetoric in the *Phaedrus* quotation cited earlier to illustrate the implicit sense of right measure in *kairos*. Plato was responding to the sophistic concept of rhetoric in the *Phaedrus*. He did repudiate the sophistic basis of probability and some of the sophistic conceptions of mechanical structure and organization, but he did not repudiate the thoroughly Gorgian idea of *kairos* as being the cornerstone of rhetoric. Untersteiner has fully developed this aspect of sophistic rhetoric, particularly in Gorgias.[42] Rostagni sees a heavy Pythagorean influence on Gorgias and Antithenes in their notions of rhetoric, persuasion, and the close affinity these have to *kairos*.[43]

The Aesthetic Dimension of Kairos

Levi begins his article on *kairos* in Plato with this statement, "The concept of *kairos,* as we have often observed, is both an ethical and an aesthetic concept."[44] He goes on to point out that throughout Greek thought the ethical and the aesthetic are consistently intertwined. Indeed, he devotes half of his article to an analysis of the beautiful in Plato and to its relationship to the good. The common basis of Plato's ethics and aesthetics is the concern for "right measure;" this had formed the popular and philosophic basis for these areas throughout Greek history.[45] And "right measure" is intimately connected with *kairos,* as we indicated earlier. Plato had summarized the relation of the beautiful to the good and to the proportionate near the end of the *Timaeus:* "Everything that is good is fair, and the fair is not without proportion; and the animal which is to be fair must have due proportion."[46]

42. Untersteiner, pp. 119–120, 194–205.
43. Rostagni, pp. 160–168.
44. Levi, "Concetto," p. 93.
45. Ibid., pp. 110–114.
46. Plato, *Timaeus,* trans. Benjamin Jowett, 87c.

More even than Plato, however, Gorgias had asserted the necessity of *kairos* for a theory of aesthetics, a topic that has been given considerable attention by Untersteiner.[47] And, in discussing Pindar's epistemology of *kairos,* we saw that it was difficult to separate it from his theory of poetry. Finally, the residue of *kairos* in Cicero, the notion of propriety, is at the basis of his entire theory of style, particularly in the *Orator.*

The Civic Educational Dimension of Kairos

The educational implications of the various dimensions of *kairos* are obvious, and they were not lost on the Greeks. On this issue, three considerations, central to my general thesis, must be made. Throughout the period that we have been considering, *kairos* was closely aligned with education. We have only to remind ourselves of the early maxims of Hesiod and Solon on the topic. In addition, we know that Pythagoras had oriented his training in education to civic education, to training for public affairs, for life in the polis.[48] Iamblichus in his *Life of Pythagoras* states: "They say that he would have been the inventor of all civic education [*politike paideia*]."[49] The constant theme of all of his speeches was virtue, with *kairos* the determining principle in each case.[50] For the Greeks, the importance of the city was the common bond of humanity that it afforded those living together and the strangers who visited them. In fact, the origins of the concept of "humanity" are traced by Fritz Wehrli to this idea, grounded in the existence of the polis.[51] Since freedom and the ability to persuade and be persuaded are the essence of the polis, it is not surprising to see the education to the life of the polis grounded in persuasion and to see this closely related to the notion of *kairos.* Gorgias, for in-

47. Untersteiner, pp. 185–194.
48. Rostagni, p. 188.
49. Quoted in Rostagni, p. 71.
50. Ibid., p. 193.
51. Fritz R. Wehrli, "Vom antiken Humanitätsbegriff," *Theoria und Humanitas: Gesammelte Schriften zur antiken Gedankenwelt* (Zurich: Artemis Verlag, 1972), pp. 12–14.

stance, relates the sense of *philanthropia* to persuasion, which was, as we have noted, for him necessarily grounded in *kairos*.[52] Probably the most obvious connection of *kairos* to civic education, however, is a symbolic one. Since the Greeks deified many of their ideals, it is not surprising that Kairos was also a god. The usual representation of Kairos was as an ephebe, a young man attending the two years of required civic and military education, at the end of which rite of passage he came into manhood (*ephebeia*).[53] The young athletic man was characterized by a striking hair style, a lock at the front with short hair behind. The presence of the forelock, says Delling, "confirms the fact that even religiously Kairos originally had the character of decision, since the lock of hair is a symbol that one must take the favourable opportunity by the forelock."[54] Kairos, the god, was thus symbolically linked to the public education program that prepared the young man for initiation into citizenship—the program, incidentally, dominated by rhetoric.

Kairos and the Contemporary College Composition Scene

As we have seen, *kairos* has distinct educational overtones in addition to its rich ethical, epistemological, aesthetic, and rhetorical tonalities. The problem in applying this rich concept to college composition is the danger of losing some of its essential complexity. Yet the attempt should be worthwhile. Indeed, it may lend a unity to several separate movements. What is required, if we are to be faithful to our historical analysis, is to devise a college composition program that will have ethical, epistemological, rhetorical, aesthetic, and political dimensions involving something

52. Untersteiner, p. 115.
53. G. Delling, "Kairos," in Gerhard Kittell, ed. *Theological Dictionary of the New Testament*, trans. and ed. Geoffrey W. Bromiley (Grand Rapids, Mich.: William B. Eerdmans Publishing Co., 1964–1976), vol. 3, p. 457.
54. Delling, p. 457.

like a notion of contemporary practical relevance to the young women and men of today. Can we write such a program? I believe that we can. And, to make this more than just an exercise in imaginative antiquarianism, I believe it will be significantly superior to the vast majority of composition programs in existence in the colleges of this country at the present time.

The Situational Context: College Composition as Rite of Passage

In an article I once wrote for *Freshman English News,* I claimed that college composition particularly, and the college experience generally, was the basic rite of passage for the most influential segment of the American populace, incorporating all of the components of Van Gennep's anthropological study.[55] I stand by the same argument today. The college experience is students' initiation into adulthood. The major decisions of their lives are usually made in these four years; they face financial, religious, philosophical, emotional, educational, and political crises, threats to the values of their family, their hometown, their church, etc. The god Kairos is a proper symbol for them: they must make decisions that will stay with them the remainder of their lives. And, lest the women feel slighted, I might point out that when Kairos was transferred to Italy, he graciously consented to a sex change because the Latin word for occasion was *occasio,* a feminine noun. As a result, she was a feminine goddess in Latin, with as long a history as her masculine counterpart had had in Greek.[56]

Students' decisions during college involve the values that will dictate the contours of their lives. Within this broad scene of decision making, let us look at the areas in which *kairos* will have

55. James L. Kinneavy, "Freshman English: An American Rite of Passage," *Freshman English News* 7 (1977): 1–3.

56. See Arthur Bernard Cook, "Appendix A: Kairos," in *Zeus: A Study in Ancient Religion* (Cambridge: At the University Press, 1925), vol. 2, pt. 2, pp. 862–863. This article is a delightful history of the god/goddess over eighteen centuries, as Cook remarks, p. 867.

a say. One caution before wandering into the separate areas: a college composition program need not be just a freshman composition program. Indeed, many of the major universities of the country are viewing the composition program as a vertical sequence of skills that must be monitored from the freshman year to the senior year—otherwise, as the Harvard experience has taught us, the skills may deteriorate.[57] For this reason, I am going to address a program that may span the four years of college—not just a freshman composition program. It is up to the individual school to make up its own mind about the sequencing of the components of its composition program. Some elite institutions may not require a freshman year; others may require monitoring at each year with a required course. Some may not find it necessary to require any course at all. But the same basic skills should result from all programs—assuming that we are sending our students out into the personal, political, and career worlds of their choice.

Kairos: Its Epistemological Consequences

What happens when *kairos,* that is, situational context, dominates a composition program? Figure 5–1, Levels of Emphasis in Composition Programs, may clarify this issue. The diagram attempts to show the various levels that may be chosen as the central point of emphasis in composing and in interpretation, the other side of the composing process, as Friedrich Schleiermacher pointed out.[58] In composition, the dominant emphasis in this country today is still the text. The "theme" is the god of the composition teacher, just as the literary text is the god of his literary counterpart, the new critic, still the prevailing power in most English departments. We are literary and rhetorical protes-

---

57. The summary report by Derek C. Bok, "Harvard University: The President's Report," *Harvard University Gazette,* vol. 73, no. 24, March 17, 1978, p. 5 [Insert, pp. 1–12].
58. Friedrich Schleiermacher, cited in Hans-Georg Gadamer, *Truth and Method,* trans. G. Barden and J. Cumming (New York: The Seabury Press, 1964), p. 167.

tants. I am urging us to move to the next bracket of the figure, situational context, where, as has been shown earlier, Plato and the sophists and Aristotle and Kenneth Burke and James Britton recommend a program based on the current life situation of the writer.

An even worse level of emphasis would be to concentrate on levels below the text. Some composition programs, such as the sentence combining program of Daiker, Kerek, and Morenberg, do just that.[59] And some remedial programs that focus only on grammar represent similar dangerous concentrations.

For the average student in the typical four-year, private or public institution, what should an emphasis on situational context mean? It ought to mean that the student do at least some writing in the area of his or her interests, that is, his or her major, regardless of what it is: physics, mathematics, English, accounting, etc. This means that some sort of writing across the curriculum ought to be incorporated into every composition program that purports to respect the situational context of the student's personal interests and career choices. Writing across the curriculum might be handled in the courses of the student's major, as happens in the program at Michigan and elsewhere, or it may be carried out in a centralized English or rhetoric department, as happens at Maryland and Texas and Brigham Young, for example. But it should be handled somewhere.

This conclusion does not rule out other types of writing, such as those traditionally pursued in required literary courses, but it at least gives coordinate legitimacy to courses in writing across the curriculum.

The obligation to write about a specific subject matter forces the student to take general rhetorical principles and apply them to a particular field. It satisfies Tillich's criteria of historical relevance,

59. See Donald Daiker, Andrew Kerek, Max Morenberg, "Sentence Combining and Syntactic Maturity in Freshman English," *College Composition and Communication* 19 (February 1978): 36–41.

Figure 5-1. Levels of Emphasis in Composition Programs

COMPOSING   INTERPRETING

UNIVERSAL HISTORY
                             Dilthey, Von Ranke,
                             Hegel, Gadamer

CULTURAL CONTEXT
                             Heidegger, Bultmann,
                             Jonas, Dilthey

SITUATIONAL CONTEXT
Sophists, Plato,   Schleiermacher,
Aristotle, Burke,   Hirsch, Bitzer,
Britton, Kinneavy   Pratt, Tillich

TEXT
D'Angelo, Moffet,   Luther, Many
McCrimmon   Critics
PARAGRAPH
Christensen

SENTENCE
Christensen,   Ricoeur,
Morenberg et al.   Genette

WORD

MORPHEME

PHONEME
Structural
Linguists

Source: James L. Kinneavy, "The Relation of the Whole to the Part in Composition and in Interpretation Theory," in *Linguistics, Stylistics, and the Teaching of Composition*, ed. Donald McQuade (Akron, Ohio: Language and Style, 1979).

interest in the subject, and free decision, but it does not solve the value and ethical issues raised by the concept of *kairos*.

Kairos: Its Ethical Consequences

Let us therefore turn to the ethical consequences of informing a composition program by the notion of *kairos*. If a writing program is to have an ethical dimension, it must take into account the value system of the situational context of the writer and reader. Consequently, the writing in a computer science department must not just be about the mechanics of creating better programs or better computers; it must look at the values implicit in the discipline of computer science and at the place of the computer scientist as a person and as a scientist in the world determined by those values.

A *kairos* program will demand, therefore, that the student write some papers about the ethical concerns of his or her personal interests and career choices. Consequently, there will have to be a humanistic component to such a program. It cannot simply be a course in what is traditionally called "technical writing," although it should include such writing.

The ethical consequences of emphasizing the life situation of the student in writing entail both individual and social affairs. The student should be asked to inquire into the aspects of his or her discipline that will morally affect the student's decisions in the present and in the foreseeable future. Such inquiries are not usual in the present university structure. Physicists leave it up to the philosophers or theologians in an institution to teach ethics, even the ethics of science. This would be all right if we could be assured that all students were being asked to write about their own discipline in such a class. The ethics issue parallels the rhetorical issue—it must be done somewhere. In any case, physicists eventually have to make moral decisions; no one can abrogate his or her own responsibilities and leave morality to philosophers or theologians.

Kairos: Its Social Consequences

The ethical issues have already hinted at the social issues; it is questionable if there is any ethic in a social vacuum anyway. Consequently, the next dimension of a writing program based on situational context must frame the social context of the writer and the reader. This dimension is an echo of the civic education component of Greek education and of the awareness of the historical-consciousness emphasis of Tillich.

Let me illustrate this dimension by an incident that happened recently. I was teaching a course in freshman composition, and I had asked the students to read an essay by Lt. Colonel Donald Gilleland entitled "The Perils of a Nuclear Freeze," which I had photocopied from that month's issue of *Vital Speeches*.[60] Several of the students were quite impressed by Lt. Colonel Gilleland's strong statements that the United States would not drop the first bomb in a nuclear war. They were concerned that Russia would, and consequently accepted Gilleland's main thesis. One student, discussing her analysis of the speech in a conference with me, was totally taken aback when I informed her that the only nation that had ever dropped a nuclear bomb in war was the United States: she had never heard of Nagasaki or Hiroshima. This student obviously did not have the historical consciousness to write on the topic.

Such ignorance of history is frightening. It is this sort of lack of fundamental information that led me to suggest to the President's Commission on Excellence in Education that all high school seniors be required to write an extemporaneous essay on a current political topic as a graduation requirement and that all colleges require a similar essay as an entrance examination.

In any case, a serious writing program should include in it some writing by the students on the political issues relevant to their own disciplines and on the political scene generally. This is one of the fundamental purposes of both public and private education. Soci-

60. Vol. 49, June 15, 1983, pp. 514–517.

eties invest in education for some social return on their investment.

Sometimes society may not like the return it gets. The social
and political consciousness of college students during the 1960s
was not the social return that many parents expected on their
investment. But at least the students had, precisely because of
their personal stake in the war, a sense of historical consciousness.
It would be desirable if they had it without the necessity of the
rhetoric of a war.

Kairos: Its Rhetorical Consequences

Sometimes the word "rhetoric" is used in the general sense of
effectiveness, or a general study of techniques of composition, and
sometimes it is used in the rather specific sense of the type of
persuasion seen in political speeches, legal pleas in a courtroom,
advertisements, and religious sermons. Thus far in this essay I
have not felt it important to distinguish between these two uses.
However, in this section I will restrict my use of the term to the
latter meaning, the historical meaning of rhetoric that distinguishes it from poetry on the one hand and scientific or expository
prose on the other. The distinctions are implicit in the liberal arts
tradition where grammar (the study of literature) is distinguished
from logic and dialectic, and all three of these from rhetoric (persuasion in this narrower sense). Up to now, no consideration has
been given to the specific kind or kinds of writing that should be
expected in a writing program. Most of the implications have
been in the direction of expository writing. Normally students in
physics or accounting would be expectecd to write informative or
demonstrative prose about physics or accounting. And even student inquiries into the moral aspects of computer sciences or
chemistry or geology would be exploratory or dialectical. All of
these would be in the area of expository writing.

Most of the university courses giving some attention to writing
emphasize expository writing. In a few courses some attention is
given to the belletristic (creative writing, drama, some journal-

ism). But few courses consciously pay attention to the persuasive as distinct from the other two. (Advertising and, in seminaries, sermon writing may be the only exception.) This alienation of rhetoric from the university at large has had some unfortunate consequences. In the first place, it has had the effect of breaking up the major connection of the humanities to the daily life of the average citizen of the state. Rhetoric, more than literature and more than science (the grammar and logic of the traditional arts), was the linking bridge of the humanities to the average citizen. By alienating rhetoric from the academy, the university has lost its major contact with real life, in the view of the populace. This partly explains the university rebellions in this century in France, Germany, and in this country. The academic can become, well, academic.

Secondly, the alienation of rhetoric from the university has produced a new exemplar of the teacher since the Renaissance. The reduction of the training of the student writer to an expertise in expository writing (demonstrative, informative, and exploratory prose) has narrowed the conceived audience to peers or superiors and separated the student's ethical and moral responsibilities from scientific concerns. Once scientist/teachers no longer feel that it is their duty to address the populace in rhetorical genres, and once they are able to pursue their scholarly interests untrammeled by the intervention of religious or moral beliefs, they can perform amorally in the laboratory and in the classroom, as mere scientist/teachers.

Such scientist/teachers can pass on to intermediaries, political or journalistic or marketing, the responsibility of using the objects of their scientific research, since they are no longer responsible to the populace directly. And such scientist/teachers will turn out similar scientist/students.

Yet it does seem immoral for a discipline as a whole to disavow the responsibility for its creations. Computer scientists, chemists, philosophers, journalists, novelists, and engineers, *as social groups,* have a responsibility for the abuses to which society puts their products, just as they also have a right to the plaudits that follow their successes. It is precisely the chemist or the computer scientist personally who can most accurately foresee the beneficial and harmful uses to which their inventions may be put. Each profession as a subculture has a rhetorical obligation to alert the culture as a whole to new benefits and also to new dangers.

This informative and rhetorical function of the profession should be taught the practitioners of that métier. In a practical vein this means that the politics, the ethics, and the rhetoric of a profession ought to be a part of the curriculum of any discipline. And the rhetoric of the discipline means the ability to address the populace in persuasive language that will be listened to. And this persuasive language will often have to be intensive, even impassioned, audienced based and biased, and stylistically appropriate to a given subculture. We don't teach our majors this kind of prose.

Consequently, it is not enough to teach the practitioners of a given craft how to communicate with each other in the jargon of their own department. They must also be taught the common language of humanity in its full rhetorical scales. This means that all disciplines should incorporate a training in the persuasive techniques of rhetoric. Thus, at least some geologists, some pharmacists, some civil engineers, some political theorists, etc., should engage in the impassioned and simple prose that affects the multitude. Training these future professionals to write only expository prose is training them to ignore their political and ethical responsibilities.[61]

It should be fairly palpable by this time that the rhetorical consequences of a *kairos* theory of composition are not unconnected with the ethical and political consequences discussed earlier.

The critical element in applying *kairos,* or situational context, to any discussion of composition problems was made by Plato in

61. These remarks on rhetoric have been drawn from an article I wrote that appeared in the Winter 1983 edition of the *ADE Bulletin,* published by the Modern Language Association.

his discussion of the place of *kairos* in rhetorical theory. The theory is only theory until it has been applied to a concrete situation with unique circumstances. For this reason it is desirable, in rhetorical (and scientific and literary) writing, to enable the students to find a realistic audience, apart from the teacher, if this is at all possible.

Real publication of the students' papers, in any local or state or national medium, directed to real audiences for specific purposes, is ideal for any composition program. I once had all of the pharmacists in Austin worried about the implementation of a legislative bill mandating the public display of generic prices for drugs because some of my students were working on a paper in this field and had contacted enough of the local druggists to arouse concern. (It helped that the state agency was also involved in investigating the same issue.) Campus publication in the school newspaper is also a wonderful stimulant. Even class publication, with everyone reading everyone else's paper, is a good technique. There is no more immediate application of the principle of *kairos* than establishing a real audience distinct from the classroom situation.

Kairos: Its Aesthetic Consequences

I wish I knew more about the subtle connections among the ethical, the rhetorical, and the aesthetic in Greek thought. I wish I really understood more than I do what the Greeks meant by beautiful/goodness (*kalokagathia*), that peculiar Greek combination of the beautiful and the good. If I did, I feel fairly certain that my aesthetic corollary of the idea of *kairos* would be more complex and more interrelated with the remainder of this essay than what I am going to suggest. I am not going to apologize for this segment of a *kairos* program, but I do feel that it could be stronger.

It seems clear that a *kairos* program of composition ought to have an aesthetic component. Levi, in particular, insisted on the aesthetic element in *kairos*. It is an educational commonplace that the aesthetic sense in the Greeks was fostered, among other sources, by the study of Homer and later by the study of the other great literary giants of Greek thought. If we are to take a cue from the Greeks to foster a sense of *kairos,* then we might do well to train to *kairos* by a study of literature.

Such a study would certainly incorporate the aesthetic into the composition program. It could be a part of the composition program in two different ways: students could study great literature and write about it, or they could try to write original literary pieces of their own. Both of these approaches have traditionally been a part of composition programs. The aesthetic might also be served by having students write about other fine arts, such as drama, dance, music, sculpture, and painting. The advantage of literature over these other fine arts is that students bring to literature a sophistication in language that permits a richer and more complex aesthetic experience.

This represents the final dimension of a *kairos* program in composition. I believe that it has its own internal defense: the ethical, the epistemological, the rhetorical, the educational, and the aesthetic foundations have a validity of their own. But two other arguments might be adduced to buttress this "kairotic" unity.

The first has already been implied. Because *kairos* has much in common with situational context, the general arguments for the importance of situational context in anthropology, in hermeneutics (literary, biblical, legal, and philosophical), in linguistic pragmatics, in speech communication, in tagmemics, in poststructuralist literary criticism, in Freud, in Kenneth Burke, and in E. D. Hirsch apply to rhetorical studies as well.[62]

The second argument has not yet been broached. Because the concept of the program that was delineated includes an emphasis on expositiory prose, on rhetorical prose, and on a study of literature, the program can be said to include the three kinds of thinking represented by the traditional liberal arts: grammar, rhetoric, and logic/dialectic. The writing of expository prose sharpens scientific thinking; persuasive prose sharpens rhetorical thinking;

62. See notes 18 through 20 for the references.

and literary analysis sharpens aesthetic thinking. The university is supposed to train students in these three basic kinds of thinking, and it is this emphasis that makes the program a continuation of the long history of the liberal arts tradition. A *kairos* program is a liberal arts program in the historic sense of the term.

The wholesomeness of the student who was scholar, and rhetorician, and aesthete is a wholesomeness we cannot dispense with. Fragmented scholars, whether teachers or students, are irresponsible scholars, as capable of turning out iniquitous monsters as beneficent marvels.

William A. Wallace

6 *Aitia*: Causal Reasoning in Composition and Rhetoric

The task to which I shall address myself in this essay is a description of causal argument and scientific questioning as these relate to written exposition and persuasion. The focus of the conference and of this volume is "classical rhetoric," and on this account I shall use as my primary source Aristotle's *Rhetoric* and attempt to mine it, to dig into it, and to rediscover in it elements that might be useful for freshman composition. Let me start, however, with a disclaimer. My field is not English, and I have never taught a course in English composition—although I was subjected to one many, many years ago, which I do not remember especially fondly. My sole credential for addressing this conference is my knowledge of Aristotle, for I have worked on his *Organon* (or tools of reasoning) for most of my intellectual life.[1] My theme is *aitia*, a Greek word that translates into Latin as *causa* and into English as cause,

1. The *Organon*, a Greek word meaning instrument, is a general term that is usually applied to Aristotle's logical writings. It includes his *Categories*, treating of ways of classifying concepts, his *On Interpretation*, concerned with the proposition, and his *Prior Analytics*, explaining the various forms of argumentation, particularly the syllogism; to these are commonly added his *Posterior Analytics*, whose focus is scientific reasoning, and the *Topics* and *Sophistical Refutations*,

although sometimes it takes on the connotation of case, in the sense of "making a case" for someone or something.[2]

Now *aitia* is not a common theme for those working on the *Rhetoric*. Enthymeme and example quite obviously are, and so is sign, as well as the famous triptych *logos, ethos,* and *pathos*. Causes seem to pertain more to the subject of scientific explanation, for they are treated by Aristotle in his *Physics* and *Metaphysics* and from a methodological point of view in his *Posterior Analytics*.[3] I have often taught these tracts, and they are difficult. Causes, as it turns out, are not easy to discover; they require an astute mind, one trained in specialized subject matters and able to discern connections, to be properly appreciated.[4] How, then, can they be useful to freshmen, who for the most part lack specialized knowledge and in whom the light of intellect is just about dawning?

Yet most books on freshman composition do treat, if only briefly, of cause and effect as a *topos* of invention, and it is quite common for them to include long sections on induction and deduction—mental processes that make at least implicit use of effect-to-cause or cause-to-effect reasoning. Moreover, Aristotle's four questions—"Is it?" "What is it?" "Has it any attributes?" and "Why has it these attributes?"—have long been regarded as stimulating thought on any subject.[5] Cicero and the Roman rhetoricians employed the first three, in a technique known as *stasis* or

---

concerned with probable argument. Scholastics such as Thomas Aquinas included in the *Organon* two additional works: the *Rhetoric,* concerned with persuasion when proof is not possible, and the *Poetics,* whose aim is to convince on the basis of a particular representation or portrayal.

2. For a complete survey of the ways in which cause has been used in intellectual discourse, particularly in relation to scientific explanation, see my *Causality and Scientific Explanation,* 2 vols. (Ann Arbor: University of Michigan Press [1972 and 1974]; reprinted Washington, D.C.: University Press of America, 1981).

3. See particularly *Physics,* Bk. 2, chap. 3; *Metaphysics,* Bk. 5, chap. 2; and *Posterior Analytics,* Bk. 2 chap. 11.

4. Part of the reason for the rejection of causal explanation in modern thought, as documented in vol. 2 of *Causality and Scientific Explanation,* is the difficulty of identifying causes in the particular subject matters with which science has been concerned.

5. *Posterior Analytics,* 89b20-26.

status, to determine the issue at stake in a court of law. Recent writers have shown how these questions can be a useful aid to invention in the freshman composition class.[6] Now Aristotle's questions, as Aquinas pointed out centuries ago in his commentary on the *Analytics,* all involve some reference to a middle term and thus to one or other type of cause.[7] Neither he nor any other commentator, to my knowledge, has focused on how causes may be useful in rhetorical reasoning, and it is to this investigation I now turn. I propose to investigate this subject in two parts, roughly corresponding to the double mandate given me concerning exposition and persuasion. In the first I shall treat of causal inquiries as an aid to exposition, an undertaking that will enable me to build up the *logos* part of my case. In the second I shall center on causal analysis as an aid to persuasion, which will permit me to range out into the areas of *ethos* and *pathos.*[8]

Causal Inquiries in the Work of Exposition

Two observations are in order before attempting to sketch in broad outline Aristotle's views on causes, their various types, and the ways in which they may be used to cast light on a particular subject matter. The first has to do with a view of causality that usually goes under the name of "causation," associated with the British empiricist David Hume, which departs considerably from Aristotle's understanding.[9] Hume proposed what we might call an "event ontology" wherein cause and effect were regarded as events

6. See Jean Dietz Moss, "Invention and the Pursuit of Truth in Freshman English," *Journal of English Teaching Techniques* 7 (Summer 1974): 15-21.

7. Thomas Aquinas, *Commentary on the Posterior Analytics of Aristotle,* trans. F. R. Larcher (Albany: Magi Books, 1970), pp. 163-169. This is Bk. 2, lecture 1, of the work, wherein Aquinas is commenting on the passage at 89b21-90a35.

8. The terms *logos, ethos,* and *pathos* are explained in what follows. Usually *logos* is taken to refer to the rational part of an argument; *ethos,* to the assent induced by the character of the one proposing it; and *pathos,* to its emotional appeal to the audience.

9. See David Hume, *An Enquiry Concerning Human Understanding,* sec. 7, pt. 2, for the reasoning that led Hume to adopt this position.

separated in time, the one before the other, but with no necessary connection between them.[10] His associationist psychology restricted understanding to the perception of atomic events, one might say, and thus causal connections were seen by him as based simply on a person's expectations arising from previous experiences of conjunctions of events. The bat does not really *cause* the motion of the ball, in Hume's view; all that we can know is that the ball's motion follows that of the bat, and being accustomed to seeing the one come after the other, we project our expectation into similar phenomena. It is our association of such events that constitutes causation, and of course that puts causation more in us than in things. It is not my intention here to argue the correctness of Hume's view as compared with Aristotle's. I would merely point out that one might be disappointed were one to look into a contemporary philosophy textbook, especially a work in the empiricist or analytical tradition, for an explanation of causality that would be useful for the purposes I have in mind.[11] It is particularly unfortunate that the scientific mentality—beginning with Newton and Locke and receiving definitive formulation with Hume—has so greatly narrowed the conception of cause.[12] The same scientific mentality has led to a depreciation of rhetorical reasoning on other grounds. Perhaps it is no accident that the downgrading of rhetoric as an academic discipline coincided almost exactly with the rise of modern science in the seventeenth century.

My second observation would ameliorate the first by calling attention to recent developments in the philosophy of science, mainly associated with the study of scientific revolutions, that cast doubt on ideals of rigor in vogue in the early part of this

10. For an analysis and critique of event ontology, see *Causality and Scientific Explanation,* vol. 2, pp. 38-51.

11. A classical exposition of the analytical philosopher's approach to causality is Arthur Pap, *An Introduction to the Philosophy of Science* (New York: The Free Press, 1962), which has been appropriated by many textbook writers.

12. See *Causality and Scientific Explanation,* esp. vol. 1, chap. 5, and vol. 2, chaps. 1 and 2.

century.[13] Today one often hears that all scientific results are revisable and that the most one can expect even from a scientific account is that it supply a probable explanation. My mention of the "probable" here immediately calls to mind another classic of Aristotle that he closely associated with the *Rhetoric,* namely, the *Topics,* the treatise on probable reasoning. In developing his "new rhetoric," in fact, Chaim Perelman insisted that whole sections of the *Topics*—mainly those dealing with the *topoi*—will have to be imported into the *Rhetoric* if we are to make it intelligible, and useful, in modern discourse.[14] Now the connection Aristotle saw between the *Rhetoric* and the *Topics* is that both employ reasoning based on common opinion, on common sense, and on "probabilities" that are easily recognized and generally accepted by ordinary people.[15] His accent on "ordinary people" is particularly felicitous for our purposes. We do not expect freshmen to have a sophisticated knowledge of a particular academic field, but at least we can expect of them that they think like ordinary people. (Sometimes I wonder if scientists themselves would not be more effective if they could think that way too—a topic my colleague, Dr. Moss, is exploring in her work on "the rhetoric of science."[16])

Aristotle's understanding of cause was based on the ordinary person's apprehension of the various factors that serve to explain either a thing's being or its coming-to-be. Thus a cause, for him,

13. Particularly noteworthy here are Thomas S. Kuhn, *The Structure of Scientific Revolutions,* 2nd enlarged ed. (Chicago: University of Chicago Press, 1970); and Larry Laudan, *Progress and Its Problems* (Berkeley: University of California Press, 1977).

14. Chaim Perelman and L. Olbrechts-Tyteca, *The New Rhetoric: A Treatise on Argumentation* (Notre Dame: University of Notre Dame, 1969), esp. pp. 83-99.

15. Aristotle, *Rhetoric,* 1354a1-12.

16. Dr. Moss has extensively studied Galileo's writings to show the extent to which he used rhetorical argument to buttress his scientific findings, particularly when the latter did not constitute definitive proof. See Jean Dietz Moss, "Galileo's *Letter to Christina:* Some Rhetorical Considerations," *Renaissance Quarterly* 36 (1983): 547-576. Generally the founders of modern science were much better at making their ideas intelligible to ordinary people than are scientists of the present day.

112   *William A. Wallace*

was nothing more than a defining factor or an explanatory factor.[17] Rather than see it as an antecedent event that always preceded its effect, Aristotle would allow a cause to be simultaneous and coexistent with the thing it serves to define or explain.[18] Causal investigation had for him an extremely wide range, and it is this that also commends itself to us when seeking out new strategies of invention. Within the Aristotelian tradition it has been common to systematize the entire range of causes within a four-ply structure, wherein the major types of cause are identified as the material cause, the formal cause, the efficient cause, and the final cause, although these precise terms are not to be found in Aristotle's text. Two other types of cause are frequently assimilated to them, namely, the instrumental cause and the exemplary cause. Perhaps we can gain some idea of the fecundity of Aristotle's notion of *aitia* by reviewing briefly these major types of cause for the help they will give us in our subsequent discourse.[19]

The Greek term *hulē,* meaning matter or stuff, conveys the basic idea behind material causality. A simple definition would identify it as that out of which a thing is made and somehow remains in it. The parts, or components, or elements that go into a thing's composition are its material cause in this sense. When speaking of elements, one need not think exclusively of chemical elements or of the elementary particles of which they may be composed—that is the scientist's way of looking at things. But paragraphs are the elements of a composition, sentences the ele-

17. Richard Hope consistently translates the Greek for cause, *aitia,* as "explanatory factor" in his English translation of *Aristotle's Physics* (Lincoln, Neb.: University of Nebraska Press, 1961). In view of Aristotle's extensive explanation of the ways in which causes should be used in finding definitions, to which he devotes a good part of Bk. 2 of the *Posterior Analytics,* they may equally be regarded as "defining factors."

18. *Posterior Analytics,* Bk. 2, chap. 12.

19. What follows is based largely on my *The Elements of Philosophy: A Compendium for Philosophers and Theologians* (New York: Alba House, 1977), which essentially summarizes articles on causality in the *New Catholic Encyclopedia,* ed. W. McDonald, 15 vols. (New York: McGraw-Hill, 1967), for which I served as philosophy editor. What is new in this essay is the exemplification, which follows the canons for *exemplum* in classical rhetorical theory. See especially *Elements,* pp. 100-106 and 151-159.

ments of paragraphs, and words the elements of sentences. Houses are made of wood and brick and steel; these are the stuff out of which they come into being. To say that a house is made of brick already goes a long way toward defining it. Enumerating the parts or materials that make up a whole is one of the simplest and most obvious ways of telling what it is.[20]

The correlative of *hulē* is *morphē*, the Greek term for form, which gives basic meaning to formal causality. Just as material causality focuses on stuff or parts or components, so formal causality focuses on the figure or shape the stuff assumes, on the whole that gives unity to its various parts. The Latin word *forma*, and its associated term *species* or species, mean shape or appearance; the outlines of a thing—even the silhouette of a cat or a cow—usually provides a better idea of what it is than a detailed analysis of its various parts. For this reason the form tends to be identified with the nature or essence of a thing; it tells us the kind under which the individual we are describing should be subsumed. To define a form or species we quite frequently have recourse to a larger class under which it is included, called the *genos* or genus, and the distinguishing factor that serves to separate it from others in the class, called the *diaphora* or *differentia*. To say that man is a rational animal is to define him through his form, the factor that differentiates him from other organisms and determines specifically what he is, that gives unity to his flesh and blood and bones, to his nervous system and brain, to the various powers that lie behind his cognitional and emotional life.[21]

The matter and the form are defining characteristics that are intrinsic to the thing defined; they coexist with it and serve to determine its very being. Without doubt, focusing on them enables us to give precision to the things we are attempting to describe or understand. But we need not remain content with factors that determine a thing from within; we can also search for factors outside it that made it come to be what it is, sometimes referred

20. *Elements*, pp. 103-104.
21. Ibid., pp. 102-103.

to as its extrinsic causes. The first of these is the efficient cause, the *archē* or principle from which it sprang into being, the *hothen* or source or agent that shaped it in its present form. To say of a painting that it is a Picasso conveys an excellent idea of what it is; the same could be said of Wedgewood china or a Stradivarius violin. Parents are the efficient causes of their children, for good or for ill, and every craftsman, artificer, or producer in the arts— whether servile, liberal, or fine—is the agent cause behind his production. Lightning is frequently the cause of fire, and ice expanding in road seams the cause of potholes; overeating can be the cause of obesity, and cardiac arrest the cause of death. Indeed, the most important changes and events that mark human life can usually be seen as the effects of prevenient agents or events. It was this pattern that so impressed David Hume and that impresses most of us also, for were we asked to identify a cause, in nine cases out of ten we would point to an efficient agent or other source of activity.[22]

The remaining type of cause is in some ways the most difficult to understand and in other ways the most illuminating. I refer to the final cause, Aristotle's *telos* (the root of our modern term teleology), which Aquinas referred to as the *causa causarum,* the "cause of causes." Simply stated, the *telos* is the end for the sake of which something exists or is done, or what it is that motivates an agent or an activity to achieve an end result. The main difficulty with final causes comes in identifying how they function in the order of nature. It is not easy to say what a cockroach or a fly is for, in the sense of identifying some obvious utility associated with its being. It seems less difficult, to me, to discern what a fly's egg is for, since it was apparently laid in order to produce another fly. I don't think any of us has difficulty, however, with the *telos* of a fly-swatter—or of any other artifact, for that matter. Nor do we have problems with the ends of more sophisticated human creations, such as the family, the town or local or national government, its committees and agencies such as the police and the

22. Ibid., p. 104.

military, even this conference on classical rhetoric and the teaching of freshman composition. Indeed, we are all well acquainted with the various ends and means that make up the fabric of our social and political life. Now Aristotle, as we know, wrote the *Rhetoric* precisely as an adjunct to the social philosophy set out in his *Politics*. And though college freshmen may know little of political science in the technical sense, most of their papers and themes tend to deal with subjects wherein purposes and ends and goals, and their proper or improper attainment, constitute the very heart of their discourse.[23]

So important is the final cause that a few words should be devoted to its various subdivisions. One may view a *telos* or end under four different formalities, namely, (1) under the aspect of its terminating a given function or activity, (2) under that of causing particular actions, (3) under that of being a kind of good that is sought, (4) and under that of being related to particular means. As *terminal,* the end is simply the outcome or goal of a process: in this sense, the adult fly terminates the development that began with the egg. As *causal,* the end is what is first intended and henceforth exercises a determining or causative influence over all actions leading to its attainment. The surgeon who performs an operation intends to restore his patient to health; it is this final goal that dictates every step and action that he and his assistants perform. Should the patient die on the operating table, that is the end of the operation in the terminal sense; it is certainly far from what the surgeon intended and could not be viewed as the causal factor that initiated his activity. As constituting a *good,* the end simply provides the reason why something is willed or sought. Aristotle spends considerable time in the *Rhetoric* analyzing the causes of human action in this sense, for we commonly regard happiness and pleasure and justice as goods that are desirable and that motivate us positively, whereas misery, pain, and injustice are evils we seek to avoid. This aspect of good, finally, casts light on how the end stands in relation to *means.* One's

23. Ibid., p. 105.

end-in-view frequently explains why something else is done, the "something else" being nothing more than the means to that end. A means, of and by itself, might be unintelligible if it were not referred to the end in view of which it was chosen. Ultimately, what any person sees and seeks in a particular means is nothing more than the goodness, real or apparent, of the end that motivates its choice.[24]

Apart from the ways in which ends are related to means, which enable us to speak of proximate ends and more or less ultimate ends, there are additional ways of classifying ends that are of interest. An *objective* end is a good or an objective that is directly sought, such as money and knowledge as the object of work and study, respectively. A *personal* end, on the other hand, is the person or group for whom the good is desired, for example, money for the family to put food on the table. An *actual* end is the very act or event in which the good is possessed or enjoyed, as when we say that the enjoyment of the food is in the eating. Related to these is the distinction between the end of the act and the end of the person acting: the first designates the normal purpose or function of a thing or action or the result ordinarily achieved by it; thus the normal purpose of a knife is cutting. The end of the one acting, as opposed to that of the act, is what one personally intends in performing the act, and this may or may not coincide with the end of the act itself; thus one may use a knife for cutting or as a screwdriver, or one may pay money for work fairly done or as a bribe to keep another's mouth shut.[25]

This brief overview of *telos* and its causality shows how complex causal analysis can become when we move into the realm of human affairs and the motivations that lie behind most of the things we do. At the risk of overburdening my presentation I would conclude with two other types of cause that can assume importance in written discourse, namely, the instrumental cause and the exemplary cause. An instrument, or *organon,* is a special

24. Ibid., pp. 156-157.
25. Ibid., pp. 157-158.

type of efficient cause that depends on another cause, called the principal cause, for the effect it produces. The knife and the pen, or the typewriter, are examples of instrumental causes; in the hands of their user, each can produce effects that are unattainable by the hands alone, and yet that require the hands' action (as well as the mind's) in order, for example, to cut or write. Obviously, there are many kinds of instrumentality, wherein people use not only things but also other people to achieve an intended result.[26] Exemplary causality involves the use of a model or an exemplar in producing a result; the Greek terms are *paradeigma* or *idea,* and these convey the notion of an operative idea that lies behind a work. Every artist and architect has some such plan, and a good part of the work of an English teacher would seem to be putting ideas in the heads of students that can serve as exemplars and models on which they will base their creative work.[27]

This exploration of the many dimensions of *aitia* should already have suggested ways in which causes may be used in the work of exposition. Thus far our concentration has been on causes as defining factors and as explanatory factors, for much of exposition is concerned with definition and explanation. We can see this if we consider again Aristotle's four questions and spell out their relationships to the causes. Simplifying somewhat, we can hold that all exposition consists of saying something about a subject: if we label the subject S and what we say about it P, then all exposition reduces basically to a statement of the form "S is P."

In this setting, Aristotle's first question—"Is it?"—is a question about S. Usually a person would not start to write about a subject that is nonexistent, and thus the propriety of this first question may itself be questioned in the normal case. Yet a student might wish to write a paper on UFOs, and should he do so the very existence of these objects becomes his major concern. Here his reasoning assumes the form of effect-to-cause discourse; he has to adduce unexplained atmospheric phenomena and show how these

26. Ibid., pp. 104-105.
27. Ibid., pp. 105-106.

demand (or do not demand) the existence of a cause that has hitherto been unobserved and thus is unidentified, the so-called UFO.

Aristotle's second question—"What is it?"—focuses on the *P* rather than on the *S* and inquires what predicates as defining factors can be seen as going with *S* to make its nature clear. There are many kinds of definition, to be sure, and the techniques for exploring their possibility are amply laid out by Aristotle in his *Topics.*[28] There, however, he concentrates on what I have referred to as a definition in terms of the formal cause, trying to identify the species or nature of a thing in terms of its genus, or including class, and the *differentiae* that serve to distinguish it from others in that class. What I have been urging in this essay is the expansion of the *topoi* explained in the *Topics* to include the other types of cause. In the *Analytics,* a later work than the *Topics,* Aristotle goes on to show how all four causes can profitably be used in the work of definition.[29] Once students understand the various kinds of cause, and perhaps work from a schema illustrating and exemplifying them, they should have little difficulty defining their subject in terms of *all* the factors that make it be what it is.

The third question—"Has it any attributes?"—really gets to the heart of expository discourse, for this puts the *S* and the *P* together and inquires what can truthfully be said about the subject at hand. It is here that Aristotle's long disquisition on ways of predicating in the *Topics,* and the *topos* of property as opposed to that of mere accident, assume some importance.[30] Dialectical inquiry operates in a framework that allows the possibility of either *"S* is *P"* or *"S* is not *P,"* but ultimately it marshals the evidence that induces assent to the one or the other—usually on the basis of how *S* has been defined. There are other nuances that are discussed in the *Rhetoric,* however, and that are closer to our concerns, but I will

28. See particularly Bk. 6 of the *Topics;* Bks. 4 and 5 also include material that is helpful in formulating definitions.
29. *Posterior Analytics,* Bk. 2, chap. 11.
30. *Topics,* Bks. 2 and 5.

delay discussing them until we come to examining persuasive, as opposed to expository, discourse.

Aristotle's final question—"Why?" or, put more fully, "Why has the subject these attributes?"—is the causal question par excellence. As the question is interpreted in the *Analytics,* it is actually a search for a middle term, *M,* that can manifest the necessary connection between *S* and *P*.[31] Stated succinctly, it leads to the formulation "*S* is *P,* because *M.*" The basic logical tool that is invoked here is the syllogism, and most teachers of composition are sufficiently acquainted with this device (from their teaching of argumentation) to dispense me from further commentary on it.[32] I would merely remark that the *M*s one seeks in constructing syllogisms invariably pertain to one or other type of cause, and the better one is equipped to identify causal relationships in all their amplitude the better one will be at discovering middle terms that are useful in this type of argument.

A question may arise here as to whether, in this essay which purports to mine the contents of the *Rhetoric* (and its related work, the *Topics*), I have allowed my concern with causes to divert my attention to the *Analytics* and conflate its techniques with those that should be the major concern of this conference. My answer is that I have not done so, or at least that this has not been my intention. The *Posterior Analytics* is concerned with apodeictic or irrefutable proof, the *apodeixis* that constituted Aristotle's ideal of science or *epistēmē,* which would be accessible only to a person who could identify the complete and proper cause of the phenomenon he was investigating.[33] Although the Greek concept of science differs significantly from our own, the methodology discoverable in the *Posterior Analytics* is that of the scientist rather than that of the person of general education. Here my approach to *aitia,* however, is not that of the scientist or the

31. *Posterior Analytics,* Bk. 2, chap. 2.
32. The *Prior Analytics,* as mentioned in note 1, is the work in which Aristotle lays out his theory of the syllogism.
33. *Posterior Analytics,* Bk. 1, chap. 2, esp. 71b8-16.

technically informed; rather it arises from general knowledge that is capable of generating belief, or *pisteis,* in the ordinary person. As a matter of fact, scientists in the present day rarely make reference to causes, whereas causal terminology continually recurs in human affairs and in daily discourse. Causes in this sense are commonplaces or *konoi topoi* that either command immediate assent or favor "probabilities" most people are willing to accept.[34] And although they can be used in the syllogism, they are also very adaptable to use in the enthymeme, as I will presently show.

If what I have just said is true, a brief corollary may be drawn that will be of interest to teachers of scientific writing or to those engaged in programs of "writing across the curriculum." Students in technical or scientific disciplines tend to use jargon or to conceptualize their subject in ways that make it completely unintelligible to anyone who lacks a background exactly homogeneous with their own. Much of the time, I would even suggest, the jargon masks their own lack of understanding of what they are writing about. It has been said that a scientist, like any other specialist, does not *really* know his subject until he can express it in terms intelligible to ordinary people.[35] If so, then the attempt to rethink expository writing along causal lines, as I have been outlining them, should also prove of help in composition courses designed specially for such students.

Before leaving the subject of exposition, I would like to say a word about the correlative of cause, namely, effect, to which I have given only implicit attention thus far. Effects are almost as helpful as causes in some aspects of our enterprise, and indeed their use is touched on in Aristotle's *Rhetoric,* although not by that name. The word Aristotle uses is "sign," or *semeion,* and the related expression "necessary sign," or *tekmerion.*[36] Signs are noth-

---

34. Aristotle, *Rhetoric,* 1358a1-36 and 1359a7-29.
35. For good examples of how difficult subject matters can be treated in terms intelligible to readers of general education, consult the science articles in *Encyclopaedia Britannica* (EB III), 15th ed.
36. *Rhetoric,* 1357a24-b25.

ing more than possible effects that seem to signal the presence of a cause (note the derivation of "semaphore" from *semeion*). In the present day, the designation "circumstantial evidence" conveys much the same idea. Were we to meet a man on the third floor flushed in countenance and breathing heavily, this could be a sign to us that he had run up the stairs. We use indicators or cues of this type all the time to form estimates about individuals or situations around us. To suspect that a man had run up the stairs is nothing more than to wonder about the cause of his flushed countenance and heavy breathing. Some signs are actually effects that are convertible with their causes, such that the one could not exist without the other; Aristotle called this the necessary sign and gave as an example a woman's lactation as evidence of a recent pregnancy.[37] Perhaps there is a deeper cause of a woman's having milk, associated in some way with the secretion of progesterone and knowable only to the medical profession, but such causal knowledge is not at question here. It is a matter of common knowledge that mothers have milk to feed their babies. It is such general knowledge of causal factors that enables signs to be used, and even to have considerable probative force when bringing arguments to bear in the public forum.

Causal Analysis as an Aid to Persuasion

This concludes the first part of my presentation, that concerned with exposition; now I shall develop the points already made to show their relevance to the art of persuasion. The element that is added when we shift from exposition to persuasion is that in the latter we are more concerned with moving an audience or a readership to some kind of action or assent. Persuasion thus has the connotation of an "ought," as opposed to the "is" of expository discourse. When we persuade, we are making a case for something, and thus the paradigm comes closer to *"S ought P"* than the *"S is P"* we have hitherto been using. When I say *"S ought*

37. Ibid., 1357b15-17.

P," what I have in mind is that *P* stands in for a course of action, or for something to be made or done, itself the subject *S* of the discourse. Political matters are quite clearly of this sort, which perhaps is why Aristotle saw the art of rhetoric as an adjunct to his *Politics.*[38] And as soon as we aim to persuade, then our discourse is further complicated by the particular audience we are addressing and the image we present to that audience as persons worth hearing on the subject. I am not saying that these elements are completely lacking in exposition, for this is directed to a readership also, but they clearly become more relevant in persuasive writing. There we have to be especially attentive to the *pathos* or emotive effort on those we are trying to move, and likewise to the *ethos* or character we impress them as having. Thus in addition to the *logos* or reasoning element we have already been discussing we now have to take into account emotional and moral factors that are so many causes in producing the desired effect.

Aristotle stresses three different kinds of persuasion in his *Rhetoric,* and indeed structures that entire treatise around them.[39] These are easily recognized as constituting the three kinds of rhetoric—deliberative, forensic, and epideictic. Deliberative discourse is generally concerned with expediency, and its aim is to move its audience to action, to pursue one course rather than another. Forensic discourse, on the other hand, focuses on matters of justice and is directed to securing a correct judgment, usually about things already done. Epideictic discourse, finally, is concerned with honoring those who are particularly exemplary, and its objective is generally to promote virtue in others. Each type of discourse, on this accounting, has a different *telos* or end, which may help to explain why I spent so much time discussing the final cause. The person who would be skilled in persuasion must therefore see himself as an agent or efficient cause, acting on

38. For a clear exposition of how Aristotle saw his *Rhetoric* as an adjunct to his *Politics,* see Larry Arnhart, *Aristotle on Political Reasoning: A Commentary on the Rhetoric* (DeKalb: Northern Illinois University Press, 1981). Arnhart's commentary is followed closely in what follows.
39. *Rhetoric,* 1358a36-1359a6; cf. Arnhart, pp. 48-53.

a particular matter (the audience and its emotional state vis-à-vis the subject being discussed), so as to produce the desired end-state—either action, or judgment, or virtue. Thus the entire burden in persuasive discourse rests on the cause-effect relationship. Not everyone can be successful at this, but those who are more likely to succeed will have a good knowledge of human psychology so as to present themselves as creditably as possible, discern how people react emotionally to various appeals, and argue convincingly to show that the facts or the evidence are as they have been adduced. Many student papers incorporate one or other of these types of persuasion, as I hope to show in what follows.

Deliberative discourse concerns itself for the most part with political subjects, since these are important to all of us and yet no one course of action clearly satisfies us as the best to be followed.[40] Aristotle lists war and peace, the defense of the country, taxes, and legislation as principal problems of this kind.[41] The ends he focuses on as contributing to their solution are very general, since they motivate us all in every situation: they are happiness and goodness.[42] Everyone, whether as an individual or as a member of a community, desires to be happy, and invariably he will seek his end in the good. Goods are of various kinds, however, and identifying them and choosing among them is the basic difficulty presented by expediency.[43] It is not my intention to go into Aristotle's analysis here: suffice it to say that it is a detailed examination of the *telos* or final cause of human activity and that the definitions he develops of happiness and goodness are models of the ways in which common opinion and commonplaces can be used to clarify these goals.[44]

Epideictic and forensic discourse are less important for our purposes. The first, being concerned with virtue and nobility, also

40. Ibid., 1359a30-b18; cf. Arnhart, pp. 55-56.
41. Ibid., 1359b19-1360b3; cf. Arnhart, pp. 56-57.
42. Ibid., 1360b4-1362b9; cf. Arnhart, pp. 57-61.
43. Ibid., 1363b6-21; cf. Arnhart, pp. 69-71.
44. Ibid., 1360b4-18 and 1362a16-b9; cf. Arnhart, pp. 57-71.

has to examine their opposites, vice and the disgraceful, for these are the characteristics we either praise or blame in others.[45] Their definitions are again determined from common considerations, and they are shown to be connected with those of happiness and goodness already arrived at.[46] Forensic discourse perforce centers around justice and injustice, and on the role of law and equity in establishing what is right and just.[47] Here Aristotle raises the question as to why men ever act unjustly, an *aporia* that leads him to look into all of the causes of human action and to center on the search for pleasure as one of the most prominent motives for unjust deeds.[48]

To deal with the complex decisions required in political and legal affairs, Aristotle then launches into a detailed treatment of the characters and passions of men.[49] The emotion he examines most carefully is anger, which becomes for him the paradigmatic passion that can be used to understand all others.[50] Anger is treated in his other writings, in the *De anima* as a psychological state and in the *Nicomachean Ethics* for its moral overtones, but in the *Rhetoric* its analysis is distinctive. Here he probes the causes of the angry response from the viewpoint of how it can be controlled by rational argument, for example, by showing how the facts of the case justify this reaction or how its vehemence may be diminished by showing that the facts do not do so.[51] I was reading through this material at the time the Korean jetliner was shot down by a Russian fighter, and I was amazed at how well it applied to the polemics of the American and Soviet press. The U.S. portrayed the incident as a wanton and unprovoked attack on innocent lives, embellishing each detail to elicit gut reactions and sanctions in the free world; the Soviets, on the other hand, described the incident as an act of valor on the part of the mili-

45. Ibid., 1366a23-33; cf. Arnhart, p. 71.
46. Ibid., 1366a34-b22; cf. Arnhart, pp. 77-80.
47. Ibid., 1368b1-26; cf. Arnhart, pp. 87-88.
48. Ibid., 1368b27-1372a3; cf. Arnhart, pp. 88-89.
49. Ibid., Bk. 2, chaps. 1-17; cf. Arnhart, pp. 111-140.
50. Ibid., Bk. 2, chaps. 1-3; cf. Arnhart, pp. 114-123.
51. Arnhart, pp. 121-127.

tary, shooting down an intruder into sensitive air space that gave every indication of being on a spy mission. The facts, of course, are the key, and it is here that the *logos* of the respective arguments assumes paramount importance. But when one considers the different audiences to which the respective accounts were directed, their rhetorical force comes very clearly into evidence. All of this, I admit, seems very theoretical, and one wonders how college freshmen might put it to use in their writing. Being somewhat out of touch in this regard, I went through a list of suggested topics for papers in the 1982 edition of Maxine Hairston's *Contemporary Rhetoric*.[52] The list was revealing, for of the fifty topics I categorized, slightly more than half required mainly exposition and had little to do with persuasion, while the remainder entailed persuasive discourse in one way or another. Of the expository topics, all fitted quite well into Aristotle's four questions and the causal analysis they involved. Those of the "Is it?" type—such as topics relating to UFOs, vampires, animal communication, extrasensory perception, life on other planets, and voyagers from outer space—seemed to appeal to students with science backgrounds, and all required the use of *a posteriori* or effect-to-cause reasoning. Other topics would involve the student mainly in the work of definition, answering to "What is it?" and usually requiring a trip to the library for those who were uninformed; samples might be cybernetics and artificial intelligence, DNA research, utopias, and inflation. Using the four-ply structure of causality already sketched, a student might be able to organize the information gained around the material involved (its parts and elements), the way it is formed or structured, the agencies at work, and the end results (including the aims of researchers and planners) that would be attained. The "attributes" question, requiring an *"S is P"* type of answer, was involved in most of the topics. Some examples: "Is the earth's climate changing?" "Do machines think?" "Do U.S. prisons need reform?" "Is suicide on the in-

52. Maxine C. Hairston, *A Contemporary Rhetoric*, 3rd ed. (Boston: Houghton Mifflin Co., 1982), pp. 418-427.

crease?" "Is mandatory retirement fair?" and "How widespread is belief in astrology?" These are good dialectical problems in the Aristotelian sense, whose answers require not only factual information but also an effort at definition and thus a goodly amount of causal analysis. The final question—"Why?"—also entered into many of the titles proposed. Questions such as "Why do people gamble?" "Why were gangster movies popular in the thirties?" "Why is 'test-tube birth' controversial?" and "Why are evangelical religions on the increase in the U.S.?" clearly require a response in terms of causal factors. Most topics were phrased in "value-free" language, so that the students might see themselves as involved in an exercise of pure and objective exposition. When one considers the topics closely, however, one finds that they invariably are of interest because of the way in which they bear on human happiness and goodness, or result in some way in pleasure or pain, and thus are not completely divorced from the analysis Aristotle provides in his *Rhetoric*.

To come to Hairston's topics that more explicitly require persuasive discourse, these can be grouped conveniently under the labels of deliberative, forensic, and epideictic already discussed. The deliberative topics fell pretty well under the categories delineated by Aristotle, particularly those relating to taxes and legislation. "Income tax" was predictably included, but there was no listing for "protective tariffs" in relation to the present state of the U.S. auto industry. Titles related to law-making abounded: the Equal Rights Amendment, pesticides, wiretapping, gun control, endangered species and conservation, solar energy, sterilization, and consumer protection are representative samples. Oddly enough, there were no topics concerned directly with war and peace or with the military and the draft, and this despite ongoing debates over the deployment of nuclear missiles, the large defense budget, the state of the SALT conferences, and the involvement of U.S. troops in Latin America and the Near East. Perhaps the overreaction to Vietnam has blunted the interest of young college students in deliberations such as these.

Topics relating to forensic and epideictic discourse fared less well. With regard to the determination of justice or injustice in past deeds, no specific "case" appears in Hairston's list; other textbooks, however, include the Goldberg trial and that for Sacco and Vanzetti, and there has been renewed interest in the press in the trial of Galileo. In a general way, however, injustice was far from absent. The topics of white-collar crime, art forgeries, child abuse, the tobacco industry, gambling, divorce and the break-down of the family, neglect of the elderly, and methods of population control all center on human rights and the ways they are being jeopardized in modern culture. But although many of the titles involved some reference to vice, surprisingly none was concerned directly with virtue. I suppose that students of the present day are not given to ceremonial discourse or the writing of eulogies. It has been said that there are no heroes in the present day, and the only goal that motivates college students is the desire to make money. Perhaps we are letting them down if we acquiesce in that attitude: it would not be a bad idea, in my mind, to suggest an essay on Mother Theresa of Calcutta or another Nobel Prize laureate who might inspire them to ponder all that is involved in true human excellence and nobility.

If my preceding analysis is correct, the student addressing any of these problems that elicits an *"S ought P"* type of solution gets involved in more than the *logos* of the argument; he must have in mind the *telos* at which he is aiming, the *pathos* of his reader-ship, and the *ethos* he himself is projecting. With regard to the *telos* and its explication in terms of truth and harmony, I will leave that to the final essay in this volume, that by Dr. Bramer. Even the *pathos* and *ethos* aspects are not without difficulty, how-ever. The student is rarely functioning in a real-life situation such as Aristotle envisages in his *Rhetoric;* rather he is engaged in an exercise, an assignment, for which the most he expects is a good grade. What is the intended audience he is addressing, and what is its emotional state vis-à-vis the topic he is writing about? We might tell him to conceptualize a universal audience made up of his peers, college students like himself. But his main audience, as he knows quite well, is the instructor who will read and grade the

the paper. Here, in some ways, he is fortunate, for he can expect a reasonable equanimity in most of us on the other side of the desk in matters relating to human passion. Perhaps we should complicate his life for him and allow him to develop his persuasive skills, by proposing to him more particular audiences whose emotional background and biases and prejudices can be laid out as part of the exercise. Let him write a paper on illegal aliens, for example, addressed to migrant farm workers or Chicanos and see what he can do with that.

The *ethos* factor, to be sure, is most important, and many low grades are probably traceable to what the teacher might perceive as a character defect in the student himself. A paper may be thought poor because its logic is defective. It may employ sweeping generalizations, *non sequitur* arguments, half-baked ideas, garbled sentences, and grammatical errors beyond numbering. The facts as alleged might be all wrong or show no evidence of research or investigation. In such a case, the fault might be with the student's mental ability and previous schooling, with his *logos,* if you will, but it is also possible that it lies in another part of his being. Perhaps he is lazy, has no control over his passions, is not giving proper attention to the course and its requirements, or for some reason is not properly motivated. Should there be evidences in his writing of plagiarism or cheating that impression would be doubly reinforced. Here too the student might be advised that his persuasive effect is being gauged on other than logical grounds, that he is being measured as a whole person, and that the *ethos* he succeeds in making manifest in his composition is as causative of its grade as its content and inner consistency.

With this I have completed most of what I have to say about persuasive discourse and the peculiar ways in which causes are involved in it, over and above their use in straightforward exposition. After having treated all the matters we have discussed, however, Aristotle devotes several chapters toward the end of the second book of the *Rhetoric* to the elements and structures of rhetorical inference, wherein he goes into more detail on the *topoi,* the example, and the enthymeme.[53] These are amply treated in other essays in this volume, but I would like now to add a few remarks about how causes are related to the example and the enthymeme.

In rhetorical inference, as Aristotle understands it, the example stands in the same relation to the enthymeme as induction stands to deduction in normal argumentation.[54] Now induction, or *epagogē,* has a distinctive meaning for the Greeks that has generally been lost in modern thought. If one were to look in a philosophy textbook written in the Humean tradition, one would see the problem of induction stated somewhat as follows. How can we ever know that all emeralds are green? We can examine the emeralds we know of, designated by *e,* and if we find that e_1 is green, and e_2 is green, and e_3 is green, and so on, then we would be tempted to say that all emeralds are green. But, of course, the problem is really insoluble, since none of us can ever examine all the emeralds there ever were, are, or will be, and the very next emerald we look at may turn out to be blue. Thus true generalizations based on experience of this type are actually impossible.

Now Aristotle, having a different view of causal inference, believed that true generalizations are possible and that they can be made for the simple reason that the human mind can see the general within the particular.[55] This is another way of saying that causes are latent in their effects, and all one need do is examine the phenomenon carefully in order to see why it is so. Those of us who read detective mysteries sense the thrill behind this discovery. We may wonder, for example, about the truth of the generalization that the square of an odd number is odd. Well, let us square three to get nine, which is odd; then square five to get twenty-five, which is odd; then seven, to forty-nine, which is odd; then nine, to eighty-one, which is odd. After a few such calculations we suspect that there is something about the nature of an

53. *Rhetoric,* Bk. 2, chaps. 18-26.
54. Ibid., Bk. 2, chap. 20.
55. *Posterior Analytics,* Bk. 2. chap. 19.

odd number that requires its square to be odd also. Starting from instances or particulars, we can arrive at generalizations that serve to explain them. Note here that the *example* of the odd number casts more light on the problem of induction than does that of the emerald. Most English teachers, I suspect, know little about mineralogy or crystallography and therefore are not sure about the colors of emeralds, whereas all have sufficient knowledge of arithmetic to square an odd number. But I could take other, simpler examples to make the same point. Parents take their children to the zoo: how many giraffes do they have to see before they learn that all giraffes have long necks? Surely they do not have to know any genetics to understand that. Most of us have seen only one moon in our lives, and yet that is enough to enable us to discern that all moons shine by reflected light.

The example differs from induction in that a single case is used to stand in for several particulars that would otherwise illuminate the universal. For this reason the example must be carefully chosen in light of the background of those to whom it is proposed. In illustrating the effect-to-cause reasoning that lies behind the answer to the "Is it?" question, I gave the example of UFOs. Most readers had heard about UFOs and got the point right away. Had I mentioned voyagers from outer space, they may not have seen that what I had in mind were the possible builders of Stonehenge in England, or of the megaliths on Easter Island, or of the pyramids in Egypt. But other examples would have worked just as well. The Loch Ness monster and the Himalayan snowman, and quarks and black holes, come quickly to mind. But they are more remote in point of time or general interest to achieve the effect I was aiming at.

Another illustration might be the inductive evidence I should have adduced in order to illuminate a truth about final causality, say, the generalization that all artifacts have an end or purpose for which they are made. I could have gone through an examination of instances, such as, a chair is to sit on, a bed is to sleep on, a knife is to cut with, and so on, and one might see the universal. But there are problems with some of the instances: the chair might be so rickety as to be useful only for firewood, and the knife might be used as a paint scraper or a chisel. So the example I presented was the fly swatter. There is not much one can do with a fly swatter other than swat, whence it gets its name. That example appeals to the reader because it delights his mind: he takes pleasure in getting the point, and that is one of the ways in which the rhetor moves an audience.

The enthymeme builds on the example by making the move from the generalization to the conclusion it entails, usually by not mentioning the generalization at all.[56] It too delights the audience because it enables those addressed to supply a missing premise and thus to make a correct inference by themselves. The enthymeme is usually presented as an abbreviated form of the syllogism and is most easily explained in relation to that logical construct. The syllogism employs six terms and three propositions: M is P; S is M; therefore S is P. The three terms, S, P, and M, each occur twice and in a different proposition, and their repetition can prove tedious to reader and listener alike. As an example I might give: all substances containing free electrons conduct electricity; and metals contain free electrons; therefore metals conduct electricity. The enthymeme abbreviates that line of reasoning to say: metals conduct electricity because they contain free electrons. The form is much simpler—S is P, because M—and this is the form I have used throughout this essay. Upon hearing the "because" argument, most people are intelligent enough to supply the major premise—in this case that all substances containing free electrons conduct electricity. It is for this reason that textbooks, even those used to teach difficult subject matters, rarely make explicit use of syllogisms and employ enthymemes instead. Invariably the deduction induces assent through a causal inference, signaled by the word "because." But even this term is not always necessary. One could say, for example, "metals, containing free electrons as they do, conduct electricity," and achieve the same effect.

Persuasive discourse differs from exposition, I have argued, in

56. *Rhetoric,* Bk. 2, chaps. 22-24.

that its paradigm is *"S* ought *P,* because *M"* rather than *"S* is *P,* because *M."* The substitution of the "ought" for the "is" signals the intimation toward action, judgment, or virtue that distinguishes the three types of rhetorical argument. An example of enthymematic persuasion might be: "Jackson ought to be elected, because he is an upright and honest man who is knowledgeable about the affairs of this township." *S* here is Jackson, and *P* is his election, the outcome that the "ought" ultimately urges. The *logos* is given by *M,* the reason for the "ought," namely, that Jackson's manifest qualifications should cause us to vote for him. The argument need not, to be sure, be phrased in such prosaic form. In a more rhetorical mode one might ask: "Why should Jackson be elected? He is an honest and upright man who really knows this township." The audience is bright enough to supply the missing premise, which spells out why anyone should rightfully be elected to office. And assuming that the previous incumbent, Johnson, was just as manifestly corrupt, one might go on: "We don't need another Johnson to ruin us." Johnson here functions as an example—one that stands in for all wrongdoing that is to be avoided, and the very mention of his name arouses emotion, *pathos,* in the audience. To make the argument more effective one could conclude: "I have nothing to gain by this; tomorrow I depart for England, where I will be far removed from Greenwood." This adds the element of *ethos:* the speaker is disinterested from the viewpoint of personal gain and has only the good of his hearers at heart. The three *pisteis* or proofs are there: *logos, pathos,* and *ethos,* and each works causally in its own way to achieve the desired action and results.[57]

Throughout this essay I have attempted to practice what I preach by moving my readers with as many examples and enthymemes as possible. Let me conclude by summing up my case in enthy-

---

57. For an extensive and profound study of the ways in which causal analysis may be applied to the development of virtue and the avoidance of vice in our present-day society, see Jody Palmour, *The Ancient Virtues and Vices: Philosophical Foundations of the Psychology, Ethics, and Politics of Human Development* (Ph.D. diss., Georgetown University, 1984).

mematic form. Classical rhetoric ought to be used in the teaching of freshman composition. This *S* and its *P* connected by the "ought" is what the essay has been all about. The *logos* that follows the "because" should be easy enough to see: classical rhetoric supplies a knowledge of all the causes one can bring to bear in building up a proper exposition or a persuasive argument. Causes are the central element of my *logos,* and that is why *aitia* figures so prominently in my title.

For my pathetic appeal, I need a good example to get my readers upset about any other approach. My knowledge of the available materials is scanty, so let me make up a fictitious author, call him Kockelmeyer, who has been hypnotized by David Hume and would not recognize a cause if he saw one. We do not need Kockelmeyer: he is the embodiment of an empiricist mentality, latches on to every fad and gimmick as soon as it appears, and lacks any integrated or sustained understanding of human nature. He can only misdirect our students, frustrating the native intelligence with which they were born. The more we think about the hours we may have wasted and our students may have wasted following Kockelmeyer in his eclectic wanderings, the madder we should get. (I presume that we are already a little upset, or we would not be interested in this conference in the first place.)

And finally, I add an ethical appeal, just in case I may not have already convinced readers of my honesty and sincerity. I am not an English teacher; I have no textbook I am trying to sell. I present myself simply as a philosopher, one interested in the life of the mind, who feels that we shortchange our students if we do not open up for them the riches of the past. My attachment to Aristotle is not a character defect. He got rhetoric off to a tremendous start, and it would be a shame if the heritage he represents were lost on contemporary students.

Note that the *logos, pathos,* and *ethos* are each there, and that it is *aitia* in its various forms that binds them all together.

George R. Bramer

7 Right Rhetoric: Classical Roots for Contemporary Aims in Writing

The writer's purposes or aims, crucial in the production of discourse, have been conceptualized in many different ways. Most frequently, textbooks deal with relatively proximate aims: conveying the writer's main idea, producing the desired effect (such as explanation or persuasion), or communicating with the intended readers. Those aims are obviously important, and the writer should carefully consider each of them. However, all of that thinking may have no constructive outcome if the writer has not also identified sound ultimate aims, which should control the proximate aims. Considering fundamental human values and goals, we can reasonably say that the ultimate aims of sound contemporary discourse are to convey truth and to promote harmony. Classical thought, as well as contemporary theory, provides substantial support for that view. Student writers should be guided by it, both in establishing their aims and in identifying means for pursuing them.

I

For the sound user of language in any form there can hardly be an aim more ultimate than the communication of truth. Undoubtedly, humans pursue through language and communication the goals they seek in life, and surely the pursuit of truth has been fundamental throughout human experience. The Sophists' doctrine of skepticism and opportunism, taught in classical Greece, has been overshadowed by the Greek philosophers' quest for truth. Works on rhetoric by the greatest of those philosophers, Plato and Aristotle, reflect that emphasis on truth, and of course it is those works, especially Aristotle's *Rhetoric,* which form the foundation of our main rhetorical tradition. In fact, both classical rhetoric and modern discourse theory support the idea that conveying truth is an essential aim in sound writing.

Insistence on truth in discourse is the hallmark of Plato's rhetorical theory. Socrates declares in Plato's *Phaedrus* that "you must know the truth about the subject that you speak or write about."[1] It is clear throughout the *Phaedrus* and in Plato's other dialogue on rhetoric, the *Gorgias,* as well as in his account of Socrates's statement at his own trial, *The Apology,* that truth must be conveyed in all honorable speaking and writing, according to the Socratic and Platonic position. The Socratic dialogue depicted in Plato's writings is itself, in form and method, an uncompromising procedure for discovering and defining truth.

Aristotle's *Rhetoric* also emphasizes fidelity to truth in discourse. In Book 1 he writes, "This certainly is right reason; the man who is to judge should not have his judgment warped by speeches arousing him to anger, jealousy, or compassion . . . And obviously in a dispute there is nothing to do beyond showing that the alleged fact does or does not exist, has or has not oc-

---

1. Plato, *Phaedrus,* trans. R. Hackforth, in *The Collected Dialogues of Plato including the Letters,* ed. Edith Hamilton and Huntington Cairns, Bollingen Series, no. 71 (Princeton, N.J.: Princeton University Press, 1961), 277b, p. 522. All references to Plato's works are taken from this edition, unless noted otherwise.

curred."[2] However, some interpreters believe that Aristotle did not maintain that position consistently. In Book 3 of the *Rhetoric* he indicates that "all else besides demonstration of fact is superfluous" but that "external matters do count for much, because of the sorry nature of an audience."[3] Thus, George Kennedy suggests that Aristotle's thinking altered and that he seems to have been "departing from Plato in the direction of the sophists."[4]

Others, such as Larry Arnhart, see no weakening of Aristotle's commitment to truth in discourse and no inconsistency in the *Rhetoric.* Arnhart writes, "In contrast to the base practices of the sophistical speakers, he [Aristotle] argues, genuine rhetoric is a truly rational activity, essential for advancing the true and the just in public speech."[5] Yet Arnhart finds that Aristotle's "noble rhetorician," in certain circumstances, might have to resort to "false reasoning" and "sophistical devices" in rhetorical invention, "ambiguities" in style, and less than ideal techniques in "parts of his speech," or arrangement.[6] Whatever concessions Aristotle may make to "practical necessity,"[7] however, emphasis on the appeal to rationality through facts and reasoning *(logos)* is prominent in the *Rhetoric* and dominant in his treatment of dialectic and logic in the *Organon.*[8] Thus, the ultimate aim of truth is supported powerfully both by Aristotle's work and by Plato's thought as presented through the portrayal of Socrates in various dialogues.

The emphasis on truth and integrity as important concerns in

2. Aristotle, *Rhetoric,* 1354a, in Lane Cooper, *The Rhetoric of Aristotle: An Expanded Translation with Supplementary Examples for Students of Composition and Public Speaking* (New York: Appleton-Century-Crofts, Inc., 1932), p. 2. All references to the *Rhetoric* are taken from this edition.
3. Aristotle, *Rhetoric,* 1404a, pp. 183-184.
4. George Kennedy, *The Art of Persuasion in Greece* (Princeton, N.J.: Princeton University Press, 1963), p. 84 *et passim.*
5. Larry Arnhart, *Aristotle on Political Reasoning: A Commentary on the Rhetoric* (DeKalb, Ill.: Northern Illinois University Press, 1981), p. 13.
6. Arnhart, pp. 160, 184, 168, and 178.
7. Arnhart, p. 178.
8. See Richard McKeon, ed., *Introduction to Aristotle* (New York: The Modern Library, 1947), pp. 2-4, for a brief description of Aristotle's *Organon.*

discourse is also apparent in the work of various modern theorists. I. A. Richards has suggested that much in the classical tradition is related to the "combative impulse" and has proposed as an alternative rhetoric the "study of misunderstanding and its remedies."[9] Similarly, Richard Young, Alton Becker, and Kenneth Pike "have sought to develop a rhetoric that implies . . . that we must be discoverers of new truths as well as preservers and transmitters of the old." They contend, "It has become imperative to develop a rhetoric that has as its goal not skillful verbal coercion but discussion and exchange of ideas."[10] Although these theories are deliberate efforts to break away from the classical rhetoric tradition, they nevertheless replicate something invaluable and timeless in that tradition—namely, the affirmation that the purest discourse is that which embodies sincere and generous commitment to the truth.

Truth, of course, is elusive and does not often present itself to the writer wholly formed, ready to be communicated. Socrates, as portrayed in Plato's dialogues, probably seems to many of us today overly optimistic about the accessibility of truth. The skeptical and casuistic Sophists, on the other hand, seem too pessimistic. A relatively balanced and discriminating view might be seen in the over-all position of Aristotle, which James Kinneavy says was actually implicit in the work of Plato but not explicitly formulated until developed by Thomas Aquinas in the thirteenth century. Kinneavy finds this position in the "liberal arts tradition" of discourse aims and says the "principle of division" on which it is based "is a scale of probability." Thus,

discourse which refers to certainties is *scientific;* discourse used in the pursuit of exploring for the probable is *dialectical;* discourse aimed at persuading others to accept the seemingly probable is *rhetorical;* discourse aimed at pleasing through internal and fictional probabilities is *poetic.*[11]

9. I. A. Richards, *The Philosophy of Rhetoric* (New York: Oxford University Press, 1965), pp. 24 and 3.
10. Richard E. Young, Alton L. Becker, and Kenneth L. Pike, *Rhetoric: Discovery and Change* (New York: Harcourt, Brace and World, Inc., 1970), pp. 9 and 8.
11. James L. Kinneavy, *A Theory of Discourse: The Aims of Discourse* (Englewood Cliffs, N.J.: Prentice-Hall, Inc., 1971), p. 56.

Stated that way, this tradition reinforces some common-sense awarenesses about the nature and accessibility of truth, and it also raises some considerations about the appropriate handling of the kinds and degrees of truth which the writer possesses. Our common sense tells us that some perceptions, ideas, and interpretations are more probably true than others and that there are varying degrees of probability available to us, whether or not there is any absolute certainty. Thus, one can write more confidently and less qualifiedly about some matters than about others. And one can be more properly persuasive with one argument than with another. Probability should not be represented as certainty, nor a low degree of probability as a high degree.

Although students of freshman composition are not likely to be writing what we customarily think of as scientific prose, they will sometimes be writing about certainties, near-certainties, or high degrees of probability. At other times they might be writing about very uncertain matters, asking questions and exploring in an effort to arrive at some degree of probability or certainty. They can benefit from the classical stipulation and traditional understanding that logical demonstration is appropriate for one kind of discourse whereas exploration is appropriate for another. And awareness of the difference between certainty and probability can serve them well in their decisions and their efforts to write persuasively.

In addition to communication of the truth, the establishment of interpersonal and social harmony is a fundamental and ultimate aim for the sound writer. That view is well grounded in classical theory and practice. Further, it is reinforced and clarified by various contemporary theories of rhetoric. Indeed, the pursuit of cohesiveness through harmony may be more prevalent in human experience and in human communication than the pursuit of truth.

The Socratic dialogues depicted by Plato support the idea that harmony is one of the highest aims of discourse. In design and method the dialogue is meant to minimize adversarial roles and to engage persons of differing opinions in a cooperative search for the truth. The dialogues typically were conducted in a spirit of fellowship and sometimes were accompanied by eating and drinking. The aim of the right or noble rhetorician, as defined in the *Phaedrus,* is not to triumph over opponents but to enrich souls by leading them to new and elevated understanding. As Richard Weaver has noted, this is accomplished by combining the arts of dialectic and rhetoric.[12] That ability of the noble rhetorician is found in the guardians or philosopher-kings of Plato's *Republic,* and it is they who take the leadership in establishing unity and harmony in the state.[13]

Aristotle also has given support to the thesis that harmony is an ultimate aim of sound discourse. In the midst of making one of his strongest statements about the adequacy of unadorned *logos* in ideal argumentation, he indicates that even in those ideal circumstances "we should avoid paining the hearer," yet "without alluring him."[14] Aristotle's extensive advocacy in the *Rhetoric* of *ethos* (appeal based on the speaker's character) and *pathos* (appeal to emotion) seems meant then, in part, to discourage the speaker from giving pain and to encourage him to promote harmony. Indeed, Aristotle seems to posit that goal of harmony in his concept of political discourse. In the *Rhetoric* he advocates that, for "the stability of the commonwealth, the deliberative speaker must be an able student" of political matters, and "above all, he must be competent in legislation, for the salvation of the State is in its laws."[15] In his *Politics* Aristotle declares that the state aims "at the highest good." Indeed, he concludes that "political society exists for the sake of noble actions, and not of mere companionship." Further, he indicates that "the good *ruler* is a good and wise man, and that he who would be a statesman must be a wise man."[16] The

    12. Richard M. Weaver, "The *Phaedrus* and the Nature of Rhetoric," in *The Province of Rhetoric,* ed. Joseph Schwartz and John A. Rycenga (New York: The Ronald Press Company, 1965), p. 322 *et passim.*
    13. Plato, *Republic,* trans. Paul Shorey, Bks. VII and IV, pp. 747-772 and 661-688.
    14. Aristotle, *Rhetoric,* 1404a, p. 183.
    15. Aristotle, *Rhetoric,* 1359b-1360a, pp. 21-23.
    16. Aristotle, *Politica,* trans. Benjamin Jowett, in *The Works of Aristotle,* ed.

emphasis on noble community purpose and wise leadership in the state justifies the inference that Aristotle favors political discourse aimed at genuine harmony rather than mere flattery.

Over all, it seems, the "openhanded" spirit of classical rhetoric described by Edward P. J. Corbett could characterize the positions of Plato and Aristotle.[17] In that spirit, classical teachers and orators could strive to establish common bonds with an audience in efforts to elevate individual minds and the body politic to the highest possible levels of understanding, policy, and behavior.

The aim of harmony in sound discourse, if only implicit in classical thought, becomes quite explicit in the work of several contemporary theorists. As was indicated before, I. A. Richards set out to define an alternative to what he considered the "combative" spirit of traditional rhetoric.[18] Kenneth Burke has identified the end of rhetoric as "identification," "cooperation," or "consubstantiality."[19] And Young, Becker, and Pike, drawing their inspiration from Carl Rogers, have devised an approach in which the "goal is thus not to work one's will on others but to establish and maintain communication *as an end in itself*." They say the "Rogerian strategy places a premium on empathy between writer and reader," and its goal is "to induce changes in an opponent's mind in order to make mutually advantageous cooperation possible."[20]

The importance attributed to truth and harmony by classical and contemporary rhetoricians is not surprising. What may be surprising is the extent to which those fundamental values conflict with each other in much of human behavior, especially communication. Even the purist Socrates, as represented by Plato in *The*

W. D. Ross, 12 vols. (Oxford: Clarendon Press, 1908-52), vol. 10, 1252a, 1281a, and 1277a. All references to Aristotle's works other than the *Rhetoric* are taken from this edition, with the volume number indicated in each reference.

17. Edward P. J. Corbett, "The Rhetoric of the Open Hand and the Rhetoric of the Closed Fist," *College Composition and Communication* 20 (December 1969).

18. Richards, p. 24.

19. Kenneth Burke, *A Rhetoric of Motives* (New York: Prentice-Hall, Inc., 1950), pp. 20-27.

20. Young, Becker, and Pike, pp. 8, 275, and 283.

Republic, considered the possible value of the "noble lie."[21] As Sissela Bok explains in her book on the ethical problem of lying, "A long tradition in political philosophy endorses some lies for the sake of the public. Plato ... first used the expression 'noble lie' for the fanciful story that might be told to people in order to persuade them to accept class distinctions and thereby safeguard social harmony."[22] Aristotle also, as was suggested earlier, seems to have struggled in his rhetorical theory with the persistent conflict between the demands of truth and those of harmony. Quite likely anyone can confirm the extent and seriousness of that conflict by referring to his own observation and experience, whether in politics, business, medicine, law, education, or everyday life.

The demands of harmony between practitioners and clients in most fields, and the demands of harmony among the practitioners themselves or among the clients themselves, often conflict with the demands of truth and truthfulness. Often it is powerfully tempting to yield to pressure and to incorporate some form of deception in one's spoken or written communication. Serious dangers lie in the direction of self-excused dishonesty, and yet many ethicists support the use of deception in extreme circumstances. Bok's treatment of the problem, however, suggests that sensitive moral judgments can sharply limit the forms and occasions of justifiable deception. Her work shows how fine ethical standards can exclude moral license with language and safeguard the ultimate primacy of truthfulness.

Truth may threaten harmony in short-range circumstances, but it nevertheless seems reasonable to suggest that our long-range hope for human cooperation may rest on truth. Great international powers seem to resort to deception routinely to maintain good relations with their allies and to avoid unnecessary conflicts with their enemies. Yet frequently they seem able to benefit mutually from sharing the discoveries of science and the products of tech-

21. Plato, *Republic,* 414b, p. 658.
22. Sissela Bok, *Lying: Moral Choice in Public and Private Life* (New York: Pantheon Books, 1978), p. 167.

nology. It may not be inordinate to hope that reliance on myth and falsehood will decline as harmony from shared truth increases. Part of that hope may rest on the computer, with its revolutionary capacities for assisting humans, both in their search for truth and in their efforts to cooperate. Perhaps one may hope for ever growing approximation of the Platonic vision expressed in the *Symposium*. In that dialogue Socrates explains that increasingly higher degrees of love (harmony) produce increasing knowledge and that the upward movement culminates in the "vision of the very soul of beauty," or understanding of the truth.[23] It seems that ultimately truth and harmony, far from conflicting, should be eminently compatible and even, in a sense, the same reality. The application of that hope in written discourse would be an effort, or aim, to communicate truth while simultaneously promoting harmony. Success in that effort would fulfill the promise both of Socratic dialogue and of modern theories such as Rogerian rhetoric.

II

Students must be able to identify sound goals for each piece of their writing, ideally in the prewriting stage. They must define their proximate goals and their ultimate aims, and they must make them all as compatible as possible. They can learn from the classical rhetoricians, especially from Aristotle and Cicero in the formulation of proximate goals and from Plato in the identification of ultimate aims. As John Mackin has done in *Classical Rhetoric for Modern Discourse,* they can "try to assimilate as much of classical rhetoric as is possible or as it seems useful to do to Socratic points of view." Mackin's hope is to avoid "tendencies" that have brought classical rhetoric "loss of favor" in the past.[24]

In dealing with the writer's most obvious or most proximate

23. Plato, *Symposium,* trans. Michael Joyce, 210-211, pp. 561-563.
24. John H. Mackin, *Classical Rhetoric for Modern Discourse* (New York: The Free Press, 1969), p. 44.

purpose, to say something (or to convey a main idea), the student must formulate a sound, truthful thesis statement. There is help in classical thought. For science and logic, Aristotle identifies in the *Posterior Analytics* four kinds of questions one can ask and therefore four kinds of answers one can posit and undertake to prove.[25] Cicero and other rhetoricians have modified the questions for use in establishing the state, or *status,* of a courtroom case. The most persistent version is these three questions: whether a thing is *(an sit),* what it is *(quid sit),* and what kind it is *(quale sit).* These questions—about the fact, definition, and quality of something—need not be limited narrowly to judicial or legal matters. As Corbett has shown and as Jean Moss has further demonstrated, the questions can be used over a broad range of subjects as a means of limiting one's subject and formulating a thesis.[26] Thus, a student undertaking to write about weekend disturbances in the neighborhood might first determine whether the emphasis should be on the fact that disturbances are occurring, on defining a disturbance in order to distinguish what is happening from normal activity, or on the offensive and bizarre features of the occurrences in order to show their outrageously disturbing quality. Having made that decision, the student can formulate a thesis that embodies a definite purpose: "Disturbances occur in my neighborhood almost every weekend," or "The typical weekend occurrences in my neighborhood are real disturbances," or "The weekend disturbances in my neighborhood are outrageous." After going through that invention process, the student should have defined what to say and should have a thesis that is both clear and sound.

Another way of formulating the writer's main idea can be derived from Aristotle's *Rhetoric.* In that work Aristotle discusses

25. Aristotle, *Analytica Posteriora,* trans. G. R. G. Mure, I, 89b.
26. Edward P. J. Corbett, *Classical Rhetoric for the Modern Student,* 2nd ed. (New York: Oxford University Press, 1971), pp. 46-47; and Jean D. Moss, "Invention and the Pursuit of Truth in Freshman English," *Journal of English Teaching Techniques* 7 (Summer 1974): 17.

three kinds of oratory: deliberative, for political situations; forensic, for judicial questions; and epideictic, for ceremonial occasions. He indicates that the aims of those three kinds of discourse—
related to future, past, and present events, respectively—are to
establish specific convictions in the minds of hearers: in deliberative discourse, that something will be advantageous or injurious;
in forensic discourse, that something was just or unjust; and in
epideictic discourse, that something (or someone) is honorable or
dishonorable.[27] Those three kinds of specific aims are appropriate
for persuasive discourse, since rhetoric to Aristotle *was* persuasion, but they have applications far beyond narrowly political,
judicial, and ceremonial occasions. Indeed, Corbett says that "this
tripartite classification is well-nigh exhaustive" of persuasive possibilities.[28]

The aims that Aristotle indicates for the three discourse types
can provide students with a broad range of possible emphases in
their writing and can function very much like the *status* questions
in the narrowing of a subject and formulation of a thesis. For
example, a student writing about federal legislators' foreign travel
could ask whether such activity would be advantageous or injurious to the United States, whether past travel had been just or
unjust to the taxpayers, or whether a specific legislator should be
praised or blamed (that is, considered honorable or dishonorable)
on the basis of his foreign travel record. Any one of those questions and the answer to it could enable the student writer to limit
the subject and could point the way to a clear, sound thesis statement.

In addition to conveying a main idea, the writer's proximate
goals include producing a desired effect. In the writing process,
deciding on the desired effect may or may not be less proximate
than deciding what to say, but surely it is equally important. Does
the student want to concentrate on persuasion, in the spirit of

27. Aristotle, *Rhetoric*, 1358a-1359a, pp. 16-19.
28. Corbett, *Classical Rhetoric*, p. 39.

Aristotle's *Rhetoric*, or does he aim at exposition, an additional function very important for the right rhetorician of Plato's *Phaedrus?*[29] In making that decision, the student can attempt to identify the demands of the subject and those of the readers.

Most subjects can be given either expository or persuasive treatment, but perhaps some lend themselves more readily to one kind than the other. The principles of mathematics, the laws of physics and chemistry, the characteristics of minerals and geological formations, weather conditions, the forms of plant and animal life, human physiology—all those subjects and many more generally seem more suited to expository discourse than to persuasive discourse. But most matters for which humans are clearly responsible—the economy, consumer goods, social services, technology, medicine, education, international relations, entertainment, the arts—seem at least as well suited to persuasion as to exposition, and perhaps better suited.

Regardless of a subject's greater suitability, real or apparent, for one functional aim or another, the principal determiner of function often seems to be the reader. Reflecting on the intended reader, the writer frequently can determine whether exposition or persuasion is more appropriate. And such matters as the reader's knowledge, values, and attitudes will affect the decision. A student should not attempt to instruct college seniors who are biology majors about the basic differences between mammals and reptiles, but might (if sufficiently knowledgeable) engage them in the debate over evolution and creation. The student writer could instruct many college freshmen on the first of those subjects, but few freshmen readers would be sufficiently knowledgeable to argue the second. And if the writer prefers the evolution theory over a literal interpretation of the biblical account of creation, he would probably do well to avoid debating with fundamentalist Christian readers, although he might interest them with an informative

29. Aristotle, *Rhetoric*, 1355b, pp. 6-7; Plato, *Phaedrus*, 277c, p. 523. The phrase "right rhetoric" is from *Plato: Phaedrus, Ion, Gorgias, and Symposium, with Passages from the Republic and Laws*, trans. Lane Cooper (Ithaca, N.Y.: Cornell University Press, 1938), 261, p. 47.

approach. Clearly the characteristics of the readers can determine significantly the function, or effect, the writer will strive for.

Indeed, communicating with intended readers is a third proximate goal for the writer. And in the writing process, identification of the intended readers may sometimes be a more proximate task than determination of the desired effect. In some situations, desired effect is established before readers, as in the case of a politician who is consistent in his intention to persuade, but varies the presentation from one group of readers to another. But in other situations, as examples in the preceding paragraph suggest, the functional aim (and the thesis as well) might be withheld pending identification of the readers. In all situations, the writer's understanding of the readers is essential for full and firm establishment of sound proximate aims.

Lacking much training in psychology, the freshman writer simply must do the best he can in analyzing his readers. But he can draw some encouragement from Aristotle. The *Rhetoric* includes a brief treatment of "types of human character," which is based on "periods of life" (youth, old age, prime) and "varieties of fortune" (lineage, wealth, power, and their opposites).[30] Despite the stereotyping in that analysis, students might be encouraged to read it for some insight into humans and especially for encouragement in the vital habit of trying to understand those with whom one hopes to communicate.

Surely it is salutary to remind student writers that discourse is primarily a medium of communication. The word *communication*, akin to the word *communion*, compellingly suggests the writer's soundest ultimate aims. It is those aims that should govern not only the selection of proximate ends but also all the choices made among possible means toward those ends. And the writer has further choices to make in establishing those sound ultimate aims.

The first step toward realizing the ultimate aims of truth and harmony, it seems, is to consciously affirm the intention of striving for the noble rather than the ignoble. Beyond that worthy act

30. Aristotle, *Rhetoric,* 1388b-1391b, pp. 131-141.

of the will, however, the writer has some discriminating to do in order to refine those ultimate aims sufficiently. Indeed, the aims of truth and harmony must be matched with the writer's subject, intended function, and readers. Above all, the writer should establish clearly the kind or degree of truth that can be conveyed and should determine whether truth or harmony requires greater emphasis for the intended readers.

The aim of truth requires careful attention. Just as Aristotle identified different kinds of discourse for treating certainty and probability, writers attempting to communicate truth must establish for themselves and their readers the nature of that aim: whether it is to convey what is certain or what is probable, and if the latter, how highly probable. Past and present phenomena often can be communicated with virtual certainty, for example in writing about the numbers of women in professions as compared with the numbers of men in the same professions. Future events generally can be dealt with only as probabilities of varying degrees or perhaps as guesses: for example, weather conditions in the "Sun Belt" as a high probability; growth in the computer industry as a fairly high probability; American touring in Mexico as a more limited probability; and the fate of the Palestine Liberation Organization as merely a guess.

Value judgments present special problems, especially in a pluralistic society, where it is often difficult to achieve consensus, even on important matters such as human rights. Of course, value judgments often can be communicated with the force of certainty or probability to readers who are shown that the judgments are consistent with their own convictions. And most readers harbor convictions that are in general accord with the prevailing values of their society, such as tenets of Judaeo-Christian morality or of American democracy. Obviously, there are exceptions, such as terrorists, bigamists, and tax resisters in the United States. And less obviously, for any reader or group of readers there very well may be one value or several that they do not share with the society at large. To take an example that may seem trivial, generic references to houses as "homes" may be fine with most Americans, but confirmed apartment dwellers might take exception. They might feel quite at home in apartments, which nevertheless are seldom accorded the stature of "homes" in real estate ads or in the popular idiom. Sensitive writers do not violate truth, but rather are faithful to it by avoiding questionable cultural assumptions in their prose. But assumptions that are not seriously questionable can be incorporated with confidence.

The sensitive writer, of course, attempts not only to safeguard truth but also to preserve harmony with readers. It is difficult to imagine a situation in which harmony between writer and readers would not be desirable and thus would not be an ultimate aim. However, the demands of harmony vary according to subject, intended function, and readers. The writer should carefully consider these variables in refining his aim and should remember several principles related to them. First, the more controversial the subject is, the greater the demands of harmony are likely to be. For example, a writer would be unlikely to aggravate tender feelings when writing about rocks and stars, unless he ventured into futurism, but he could anticipate some uneasy readers when writing about social services or alcohol consumption. Second, an effort to persuade probably threatens harmony more than an effort to explain. For example, informing people about the reproduction rate of deer is unlikely to generate conflict, but advocating a longer deer hunting season can predictably arouse some hostility and produce divisiveness.

Finally, for any given writer, some readers present greater challenges to harmony than others. Consider a Republican writer and Democratic readers. Or consider an orthodox Jew and students from Arab countries. Indeed, the values and attitudes of readers can elicit divisiveness over subjects and functional aims that, for other readers, would be matters of detached interest or even boredom. Arab students, for example, would probably react very differently than most American students to an expository description of Jerusalem. The effective writer must always strive for awareness of subject, function, and reader that, singly or in combination, can threaten the harmony integral to ideal communication.

The variables of subject, function, and reader may demand varying emphases on truth and harmony, but usually the two aims must be given balanced consideration. Sometimes writers in circumstances clearly nonthreatening to their readers can afford the luxury of concentrating, in the realm of ultimate aims, exclusively on truth. Much technical and scientific writing is presumably of that kind. Similarly, writers whose readers are almost assuredly sympathetic with their message might have the freedom to slight truth without diminishing harmony. Probably some political writings would be good examples. But there are problems in the luxury and the freedom of those extreme circumstances. Although simply sharing the truth can sometimes produce harmony, there are few truths that do not have the potentiality of offending or threatening someone. And single-minded pursuit of harmony is even less promising. It is not clear that the achievement of harmony, by itself, is likely to serve the aim of truth, and it is usually possible that distortion of truth will undermine harmony. Whatever the circumstances, the writer identifying his aims should minimize neither the demands of truth nor those of harmony. Most situations that students will face will call for the pursuit of both.

I have implied two dimensions in the concept of sound aims. One has to do with appropriateness, the other with ethics. The writer's choices among possible aims are appropriate if they fit the proximate circumstances of subject, function, and reader. The writer's choices are ethical if they meet the ultimate demands of truth and harmony. The ethical dimension deserves further consideration.

The first requirement of ethical writing, it seems, is that genuine truth and harmony be pursued rather than their counterfeits. The desire to *seem* right presents a powerful temptation to distort and to deceive. The desire to *maintain appearances* of interpersonal or social accord presents the temptation to feign empathy, agreement, or esteem.[31] But accuracy must not be forfeited to overstatement or understatement, flattery must not be substituted for genuine regard, feeling must not displace thought. Because of the ever-threatening conflict between real aims and their spurious counterparts, writers must continually evaluate their motives as well as the means of their discourse.

A second ethical requirement is that proximate aims not be preferred over ultimate aims. The legitimate aim to persuade might be served more effectively in some situations by overstatement and flattery than by a truthful statement of facts. Examples from advertising and political campaigning are abundant. But the aim to persuade should not override the aim to be truthful. There is also a danger that inordinate pursuit of the legitimate aim to inform or explain could result in unnecessary damage to harmony. Consider the overzealous and insensitive classroom instructor whose indifference to the emotional needs of students has alienated the students, not only from himself but also from the very subject he so doggedly is striving to teach.

Some of these ethical problems are of concern to Socrates (and Plato) in the *Gorgias* and the *Phaedrus,* and they inform the distinction between base rhetoric and right rhetoric. However, many readers today might raise questions about the ethical vision of those dialogues. For one thing, certitude often seems less accessible than Socrates suggests. Nevertheless, that awareness does not deter rational humans from searching out at least the highest probabilities available. Another problem is that serious matters of life, death, and human welfare sometimes seem to mandate violation of truth. Sissela Bok, while emphasizing the destructive potentialities of lying, concludes that "there are at least *some* circumstances which warrant a lie."[32] Some ethicists might disagree. But in any case the view that the truth must be sacrificed, in extreme circumstances and as a last resort, should not create

---

31. Regarding this problem in the tradition stemming from classical rhetoric, see Allen Ramsey, "Rhetoric and the Ethics of 'Seeming,'" *Rhetoric Society Quarterly* 11 (Spring 1981): 85-96.

32. Bok, p. 45

defection from fundamental honesty. Bok shows "how often the justifications" invoked for lies "are insubstantial, and how they can disguise and fuel all other wrongs." She writes, "Trust and integrity are precious resources, easily squandered, hard to regain. They can thrive only on a foundation of respect for veracity."[33] A third problem is that Socrates seems to the modern reader to be too optimistic about achieving a meeting of opposed minds. A desire always to write harmoniously probably would not be realistic. Folk wisdom tells us that one cannot satisfy "all of the people all of the time." In fact, it must be apparent from casual observation and experience that the desire for truth often conflicts unavoidably with the desire for harmony in human interaction and communication. That awareness, however, does not warrant cynical disregard of the quest for deep and genuine harmony. Despite very real difficulties in striving for truth and harmony, the student writer cannot justifiably abandon either of these ultimate aims.

III

The writer should be guided in the writing process by the aims he has established. Those aims should inform his decisions during as much of the prewriting, writing, and rewriting stages as possible. Ideally, he would determine his aims early in the prewriting stage or even before it. Surely he should not begin the writing stage without a clear understanding of his goals, but he might alter one or more of them during that stage or even during the rewriting process. Whatever the case, the writer's management of content, structure, and style should reflect, in the final draft, consistent fidelity to the established aims. Both classical and contemporary works provide students with an abundance of resources and strategies to carry out not only their proximate aims but also the ultimate aims of truth and harmony.

The writer's content is the product of his investigation, inven-

33. Ibid., p. 249.

tion, and reasoning, all of which should be motivated and guided by the quest for truth. For investigation, students can be given one of many current guides to library resources. For invention, there are the *topoi* of classical rhetoric. For reasoning, there are the enthymeme and the use of examples described in Aristotle's *Rhetoric* as well as more formal methods of reasoning and inquiry explained in the *Organon*. Helpful also is Cicero's explanation that deductive reasoning in discourse might have five parts (two premises, proofs of each, and a conclusion), but that it might also have fewer than five.[34] Regarding the aim of harmony, Aristotle's *Rhetoric* and contemporary psychology recommend that readers' ideas, knowledge, and values be considered and endorsed in one's content insofar as honesty allows.

The writer's management of discourse structure, curiously neglected in some modern textbooks, was elaborately treated by classical rhetoricians. Aristotle very reasonably trimmed the multiplicity of parts in classical arrangement to the two essentials: statement and argument (in current terms, thesis and support).[35] However, the writer is left with a vital question that few current textbooks raise or answer: Which of the essential two parts of discourse comes first? Whereas tradition has it that the thesis usually comes first, in some situations the demands of harmony recommend that support or demonstration precede the main point. There is precedent for the latter approach in the Socratic dialogue, which proceeds step by step through layers of reasoning to the main proposition near the end.

The third area to be considered, the writer's style, has been extensively treated both in antiquity and in our time. Plato and Aristotle expressed a preference for relatively plain style, which might be considered more appropriate than elaborate or embellished style for reasoned, truthful prose and perhaps also for prose

---

34. Cicero, *De Inventione,* in *De Inventione De Optimo Genere Oratorum, Topica,* with an English translation by H. M. Hubbell, The Loeb Classical Library (Cambridge, Mass.: Harvard University Press, 1949), vol. 1, pp. xxxiv-xli, pp. 99-123.

35. Aristotle, *Rhetoric,* 1414a, p. 220.

meant to produce harmony.[36] The Committee on Public Doublespeak of the National Council of Teachers of English frequently
cites examples of prose that employ obscure jargon, evasive eu-
phemism, and tortuous syntax—all for the apparent purpose of
concealing or distorting the truth.[37] From the Committee's publications and other current sources one can identify some of the
probable features of truthful, harmonious style: relatively denota-
tive, concrete, and literal words; properly qualified assertions;
avoidance of rhetorical questions; freedom from abnormalities in
sentence length and structure; avoidance of sarcasm and ridicule.
Not everyone will agree on all those features and the Committee
itself employs one of them, ridicule, in its celebrated annual "Doublespeak Award." But the list does seem promising, not only for the
communication of unbiased truth but also for the preservation of
harmony between a writer and his readers or his opponents.

These ancient and modern resources for handling the elements
of discourse are a limited sample of the means available to writing
students in their pursuit of sound aims, both proximate and ultimate. More thorough consideration of the writer's means is matter for other discussions. Let us merely say that students' writing
should be accurate and logical in content, solid and tactful in
structure, clear and considerate in style. To help students we can
draw on classical rhetoric and philosophy as well as contemporary
discourse theory. We can also supply them with appropriate real-
life models and devise assignments that require thorough
identification of sound controlling aims.

· IV

Science and technology have made our world very different
from the world of classical Greece and Rome, but ultimate human

36. Plato, *Gorgias,* trans. W. D. Woodhead, 449b-449c, pp. 232-233; Aristotle,
Rhetoric, 1404a-1404b, pp. 184-185.
37. See the *Quarterly Review of Doublespeak;* Hugh Rank, ed., *Language and
Public Policy* (Urbana, Ill.: National Council of Teachers of English, 1974); and
Daniel Dieterich, ed., *Teaching about Doublespeak* (Urbana, Ill.: National Council
of Teachers of English, 1976).

needs and goals have not essentially altered since the golden eras of those civilizations. As in antiquity, some fundamental problems for the speaker or writer today seem to be that blunt statement of the truth can be confrontational and that distortion of it is manipulative. The middle ground of cooperative search for truth, now identified as Rogerian rhetoric, was foreshadowed in Plato's portrayal of the Socratic dialogue.

Teachers should encourage writing students to resist the recurrent suggestion that composition classes are concerned merely with "skills" and that values are reserved for literature and humanities classes. High standards of rationality and ethical behavior are deeply rooted in our rhetorical tradition and are well articulated by some contemporary discourse theorists. If that body of thought seems to propose to students an unrealistic and elitist model akin to Plato's philosopher-king, one might reflect on the implications of universal education and political suffrage in our culture. Rationality and virtue are imperative in sound contemporary writing just as they were in the "right rhetoric" of classical antiquity.[38]

38. I wish to thank Professors Jean Dietz Moss and William A. Wallace, both of The Catholic University of America, for providing valuable suggestions for the revision of this essay.

Appendix I

Roster of Conference Participants

Conference Director:
JEAN DIETZ MOSS, The Catholic University of America

Assistants to the Director:
BR. DANIEL ADAMS, The Catholic University of America
KATHLEEN MILLAR IMBEMBA, The Catholic University of America

Lecturers:
GEORGE R. BRAMER, Lansing Community College
EDWARD P. J. CORBETT, The Ohio State University
MAXINE C. HAIRSTON, University of Texas–Austin
JAMES L. KINNEAVY, University of Texas–Austin
RICHARD J. SCHOECK, University of Colorado–Boulder
WILLIAM A. WALLACE, The Catholic University of America

Discussion Leaders:
ROSEMARY GATES, The Catholic University of America
LOIS M. MCMILLAN, Morgan State University
JOHN POULAKOS, Pennsylvania State University–Delaware Campus
BARBARA STOUT, Montgomery College
RICHARD E. YOUNG, Carnegie-Mellon University

Others Who Attended:
JAMES C. ADDISON, Western Carolina University
ANNE AGEE, Anne Arundel Community College
JOSEPH ALVAREZ, Central Piedmont Community College
NANCY G. ANDERSON, Auburn University
HOWARD A. BARNETT, Lindenwood College
JAMES S. BAUMLIN, Texas Christian University
WALTER H. BEALE, University of North Carolina
JOHN K. BOLTON, Montgomery College
ETHEL BRADFORD, Siena Heights College
RUTH CAROLYN BUDGETT, University of Akron
DINSHAW M. BURJORJEE, Montgomery College

ROBERT E. BURKHOLDER, The Pennsylvania State
University–Wilkes-Barre
MARIAN CALABRESE, Sacred Heart University, Bridgeport, Conn.
RONNIE D. CARTER, Indiana University, East
RICHARD W. CLANCY, John Carroll University
JOAN E. CORBETT, Fayetteville State College
DAVID M. CRATTY, Cuyahoga Community College
E. ROBERT CRONIN, Mount Wachusett College
KAREN REISER DHAR, Ellsworth College
MARY COLLEEN DILLON, Thomas More College
ROBERT DARRELL, Kentucky Wesleyan College
GEORGE DORRILL, Winthrop College
WILLARD DUNN, Indiana University
WARREN DWYER, Bradley University
PETER G. EVARTS, Oakland University, Rochester, Mich.
JEANNE FAHNESTOCK, University of Maryland
ANGELA DiPACE FRITZ, Sacred Heart University, Bridgeport, Conn.
RICHARD FULKERSON, East Texas State University
ROBERTA DIXON GATES, Southern Technical Institute
FAY T. GREENWALD, Mercy College
KRIS D. GUTIERREZ, University of Colorado–Boulder
MARY LOUISE HALL, Siena Heights College
ROBERT S. HALLER, University of Nebraska–Lincoln
CHARLES D. HARRINGTON, Indiana University–South Bend
NOREEN L. HAYES, Allegany Community College
CAROLYN HILL, University of Maryland
KATHLEEN HUNTER, College of St. Elizabeth
BARBARA E. JONES, Alabama A & M University
JAMES JUROE, Hillsdale College
CRAIG KALLENDORF, Texas A & M University
JANE KAUFMAN, University of Akron
KATHLEEN A. KELLY, Babson College
TOM KEMNE, Bellarmine College
JAMES KINNEY, Virginia Commonwealth University
EDWARD F. KRICKEL, University of Georgia
SARAH B. KRICKEL, Emmanuel College
JERRI LINDBLAD, Frederick Community College
MICHELLE LORIS, Sacred Heart University, Bridgeport, Conn.
JOYCE B. MACALLISTER, University of Richmond
WILLIAM J. McCLEARY, Genesee Community College
MARGARET McDONALD, Regis College
CAROLYN McGINTY, Rosary College

MARY L. MALANY, Regis College
MARTHA MANHEIM, Siena Heights College
CAROLYN MATALENE, University of South Carolina
ARTHUR A. MOLITIERNO, Wright State University
PAUL MONTGOMERY, University of Minnesota Technical College
S. S. MOORTY, Southern Utah State College
JANE MORRISSEY, Our Lady of the Elms College
LUCILLE MORSE, East Central State University
GRATIA MURPHY, Youngstown State University
JAMES R. NICHOLS, Muskingum College
DONALD NOBLES, Auburn University
LARRY R. OLPIN, Central Missouri State University
ELLEN OWENS, Chabot College
FRANK M. PATTERSON, Central Missouri State University
BARSHAN PERUSEK, University of Akron
BETTY P. PYTLIK, Ohio University
MELVIN RAFF, Strayer College
LINDA ROBERTSON, Wichita State University
ANJI K. ROY, University of Wisconsin
AIDA M. RUIZ ORTIZ, Hostos Community College
LEIGH RYAN, University of Maryland
ANTHRELL D. SANDERS, North Carolina Central University
ELIZABETH JAN SAVIN, Missouri Western State College
JOHN F. SCHELL, University of Arkansas
PATRICK SMITH, University of San Francisco
RICHARD L. SPROW, Westminister College
ROBERTA LYNNE STAPLES, Sacred Heart University, Bridgeport,
Conn.
BRAINERD STRANAHAN, Hiram College
RONALD A. SUDOL, Oakland University, Rochester, Minn.
SATYA TANDON, Mohawk Valley Community College
WILLIAM G. THOMSON, Olivet College
REBECCA W. UMPHREY, University of Central Florida
ROBERT E. UMPHREY, University of Central Florida
ALFREDO VILLANUEVA, Hostos Community College
MICHAEL VIVION, University of Missouri, Kansas City
CHARLES WHITNEY, The Pennsylvania State University,
Worthington-Scranton
FRANCIS E. ZAPATHA, The American University

Appendix II

Select Bibliography for Further Reading

Abelson, Paul. *The Seven Liberal Arts: A Study in Mediaeval Culture.* Columbia University Teachers' College, Columbia University, 1906. Reprinted: New York: AMS Press, 1972.

Aristotle. *Rhetoric.* In *The Rhetoric of Aristotle: An Expanded Translation with Supplementary Examples for Students of Composition and Public Speaking,* by Lane Cooper. New York: Appleton-Century-Crofts, Inc., 1932.

Arnhart, Larry. *Aristotle on Political Reasoning: A Commentary on the Rhetoric.* DeKalb: Northern Illinois University Press, 1981.

Baier, Kurt. *The Moral Point of View: A Rational Basis of Ethics.* Ithaca, N.Y.: Cornell University Press, 1958.

Baldwin, Charles Sears. *Medieval Rhetoric and Poetic (to 1400) Interpreted from Representative Works.* New York: The Macmillan Co., 1928. Reprint. Gloucester, Mass.: Peter Smith, 1959; St. Clair Shores, Mich.: Scholarly Press, 1965.

_____. *Renaissance Literary Theory and Practice: Classicism in the Rhetoric and Poetic of Italy, France, and England, 1400-1600.* Edited with an introduction by Donald Lemen Clark. New York: Columbia University Press, 1939.

_____. *Ancient Rhetoric and Poetic.* Gloucester, Mass.: Peter Smith, 1959.

Bitzer, Lloyd F. "Aristotle's Enthymeme Revisited." *Quarterly Journal of Speech Communication* 45 (December 1959): 399-408.

_____. "The Rhetorical Situation." *Philosophy and Rhetoric* 1 (1968): 1-14.

Bitzer, Lloyd F., and Edwin Black, eds. *The Prospect of Rhetoric. Report of the National Development Project.* Sponsored by Speech Communication Association. Englewood Cliffs, N.J.: Prentice-Hall, Inc., 1971.

Bolgar, R. R. *The Classical Heritage and Its Beneficiaries.* Cambridge: Cambridge University Press, 1954.

Bramer, George R. "Truth and Harmony as Rhetorical Goals." *English Journal* (September 1970): 824-833.

Burke, Kenneth. *A Grammar of Motives.* Berkeley: University of California Press, 1969.

Cicero. *Ad C. Herennium de Ratione Dicendi (Rhetorica ad Herennium).* Translated by Harry Caplan. The Loeb Classical Library. Cambridge: Harvard University Press, 1952.

_____. *De Inventione—De Optimo Genere Oratorum—Topica.* Translated by H. M. Hubbell. The Loeb Classical Library. Cambridge: Harvard University Press, 1949.

Clark, Donald Lemen. *Rhetoric in Greco-Roman Education.* New York: Columbia University Press, 1957.

Connors, Robert J., Lisa S. Ede, and Andrea A. Lunsford. *Essays on Classical Rhetoric and Modern Discourse.* Carbondale and Edwardsville: Southern Illinois University, 1984.

Corbett, Edward P. J. "The Rhetoric of the Open Hand and the Rhetoric of the Closed Fist." *College Composition and Communication* 20 (December 1969): 288-296.

_____. *Classical Rhetoric for the Modern Student.* 2nd ed. New York: Oxford University Press, 1971.

Curtius, Ernst R. *European Literature and the Latin Middle Ages.* Translated by Willard R. Trask. Bollingen Series, no. 36. New York: Pantheon Books, 1953. Reprint. Princeton, N.J.: Princeton University Press, 1967.

Enos, Richard Leo. *Plato: True and Sophistic Rhetoric.* Amsterdam: Editions Rodopi, 1979.

Enos, Richard Leo, and Howard E. Sypher. "A Bibliography for the Study of Classical Invention." *Rhetoric Society Quarterly* 11 (Winter 1981): 45-62.

Erickson, Keith V., ed. *Aristotle: The Classical Heritage of Rhetoric.* Metuchen, N.J.: Scarecrow Press, 1974.

Gage, John. "Teaching the Enthymeme: Invention and Arrangement." *Rhetoric Review* 2 (September 1983): 38-50.

Grimaldi, William M. A., S. J. "The Aristotelian Topics." *Traditio* 14 (1958): 1-16. In *Aristotle: The Classical Heritage of Rhetoric,* edited by Keith V. Erickson, pp. 176-193. Metuchen, N.J.: Scarecrow Press, 1974.

_____. *Aristotle, Rhetoric I: A Commentary.* New York: Fordham University Press, 1980.

Hairston, Maxine C. "The Winds of Change: Thomas Kuhn and the Revolution in the Teaching of Writing." *College Composition and Communication* 33 (February 1982): 76-82.

Harrington, David V. "Teaching Ethical Writing." *Freshmen English News* 10 (Spring 1981): 13-16.

Harrington, Elbert W. *Rhetoric and the Scientific Method of Inquiry: A Study of Invention.* Boulder, Colo.: University of Colorado, 1948.

Hauser, Gerard A. "The Most Significant Passage in Aristotle's *Rhetoric* or How Function May Make Moral Philosophers of Us All." *Rhetoric Society Quarterly* 12 (Winter 1982): 13-16.

Horner, Winifred Bryan. *The Present State of Scholarship in Historical and Contemporary Rhetoric.* Columbia and London: University of Missouri Press, 1983.

Howell, Wilbur S. *Logic and Rhetoric in England, 1500-1700.* Princeton, N.J.: Princeton University Press, 1956.

The Institutio oratoria of Quintilian. Translated by H. E. Butler. 4 vols. The Loeb Classical Library. Cambridge: Harvard University Press, 1920-1922.

Johnstone, Henry W. "Truth Communication and Rhetoric in Philosophy." *Revue Internationale de Philosophie* 23 (1969): 405-406.

Kennedy, George A. *The Art of Persuasion in Greece.* Princeton, N.J.: Princeton University Press, 1963.

_____. *The Art of Rhetoric in the Roman World: 300 B.C.-A.D. 300.* Princeton, N.J.: Princeton University Press, 1972.

_____. *Classical Rhetoric and Its Christian and Secular Tradition from Ancient to Modern Times.* Chapel Hill: The University of North Carolina Press, 1980.

Kinneavy, James L. *A Theory of Discourse: The Aims of Discourse.* Englewood Cliffs, N.J.: Prentice-Hall, Inc., 1971. Reprint. New York: W. W. Norton & Co., 1980.

_____. "Freshman English: An American Rite of Passage." *Freshman English News* 7 (1977): 1-3.

_____. "Restoring the Humanities: The Return of Rhetoric from Exile." In *The Rhetorical Tradition and Modern Writing,* edited by James J. Murphy. New York: Modern Language Association, 1982.

Kristeller, Paul Oskar. *Renaissance Thought and Its Sources.* Edited by Michael Mooney. New York: Columbia University Press, 1979.

Lanham, Richard A. *A Handlist of Rhetorical Terms: A Guide for Students of English Literature.* Berkeley: University of California Press, 1969.

Lechner, Sister Joan Marie. *Renaissance Concepts of the Commonplaces: An Historical Investigation of the General and Universal Ideas Used in All Argumentation and Persuasion, with Special Emphasis on the Educational and Literary Tradition of the Sixteenth and Seventeenth Centuries.* New York: Pageant Press, 1962.

Leff, Michael C. "The Topics of Argumentative Invention in Latin Rhetorical Theory from Cicero to Boethius." *Rhetorica* 1 (Spring 1983): 23-44.

McKeon, Richard. "Rhetoric in the Middle Ages." *Speculum* 17 (1942):

1-32. In *Critics and Criticism: Ancient and Modern,* edited by R. S. Crane, pp. 260-296. Chicago: University of Chicago Press, 1952, 1975. In *The Province of Rhetoric,* edited by Joseph Schwartz and John A. Rycenga, pp. 172-212. New York: The Ronald Press Co., 1965.

Moss, Jean D. "Invention and the Pursuit of Truth in Freshman English." *Journal of English Teaching Techniques* 7 (Summer 1974): 15-21.

Murphy, James J. *Rhetoric in the Middle Ages: A History of Rhetorical Theory from Saint Augustine to the Renaissance.* Berkeley, Los Angeles, and London: University of California Press, 1974, 1981.

———, ed. *The Rhetorical Tradition and Modern Writing.* New York: The Modern Language Association of America, 1982.

Ochs, Donovan J. "Aristotle's Concept of Formal Topics." *Speech Monographs* 36 (November 1969): 419-425.

Ong, Walter, S. J. *Ramus, Method and the Decay of Dialogue: From the Art of Discourse to the Art of Reason.* Cambridge: Harvard University Press, 1958.

Paetow, Louis J. *The Arts Course at Medieval Universities with Special Reference to Grammar and Rhetoric.* University Studies of the University of Illinois, nos. 3 and 7. Champaign: University of Illinois Press, 1910. Reprint. Dubuque, Iowa: Wm. C. Brown Reprint Library, n.d.

Perelman, Chaim, and L. Olbrechts-Tyteca. *The New Rhetoric: A Treatise on Argumentation.* Translated by John Wilkinson and Purcell Weaver. Notre Dame: University of Notre Dame Press, 1969.

———. *The Realm of Rhetoric.* Translated by William Kluback. Notre Dame: University of Notre Dame Press, 1982.

Plato. *Phaedrus.* Translated by R. Hackforth. In *The Collected Dialogues of Plato including the Letters,* edited by Edith Hamilton and Huntington Cairns. Bollingen Series, no. 71. Princeton, N.J.: Princeton University Press, 1961.

———. *Phaedrus: Translated with an Introduction and Commentary.* Translated by R. Hackforth. Cambridge: Cambridge University Press, 1972.

Rashdall, Hastings. *The Universities of Europe in the Middle Ages.* 3 vols. 2nd ed. Revised by F. M. Powicke and A. B. Emden. Oxford: Clarendon Press, 1936.

Schoeck, Richard J. "Rhetoric and Law in Sixteenth-Century England." *Studies in Philology* (1953): 110-127.

———. "On Rhetoric in Fourteenth-Century Oxford." *Mediaeval Studies* 30 (1968): 214-225.

Schwartz, Joseph and John A. Rycenga. eds. *The Province of Rhetoric.* New York: The Ronald Press Company, 1965.

Seigel, Jerrold. *Rhetoric and Philosophy in Renaissance Humanism: The Union of Eloquence and Wisdom, Petrarch to Valla.* Princeton, N.J.: Princeton University Press, 1968.

Solmsen, Friedrich. "The Aristotelian Tradition in Ancient Rhetoric." *American Journal of Philology* 62 (1941): 35-50, 169-190. In *Aristotle: The Classical Heritage of Rhetoric,* edited by Keith V. Erickson, pp. 278-309. Metuchen, N.J.: Scarecrow Press, 1974.

Tate, Gary, and Edward P. J. Corbett, eds. *The Writing Teacher's Sourcebook.* New York: Oxford University Press, 1981.

Toulmin, Stephen E. *The Uses of Argument.* Cambridge: Cambridge University Press, 1958.

Wallace, Karl R. *Francis Bacon on Communication and Rhetoric or: The Art of Applying Reason to the Imagination for the Better Moving of the Will.* Chapel Hill: University of North Carolina Press, 1943.

Wallace, William A. *Causality and Scientific Explanation.* 2 vols. Ann Arbor: University of Michigan Press, 1972-1974.

———. *The Elements of Philosophy.* New York: Alba House, 1977.

Walter, Otis M. "The Value of the Classics in Rhetoric." *College Composition and Communication* 32 (December 1981): 416-422.

Young, Richard E., Alton L. Becker, and Kenneth L. Pike. *Rhetoric: Discovery and Change.* New York: Harcourt, Brace and World, Inc., 1970.

Index

Académie Française, 37
Accidents, 15
Ad Herennium, pseudo-Cicero, 4,
    29, 31, 35
Adams, Daniel, viii
Adler, Mortimer, 56
Aesthetics, 18, 81, 91–92
Aim(s): proximate, 21, 135,
    145–148, 151; ultimate, 21, 135,
    139–143, 148–155. *See also*
    End(s); Cause: final (*telos*)
Aitia, 1, 17–19, 109–133. *See also*
    Cause(s); Causality
Alcuin, 33
Antisthenes, 87, 91
Appropriateness (*kairos*), 80,
    82–88, 90–93, 146, 150
Aquinas, Thomas, 26, 108–109,
    138
Aristotle, 3, 13–16, 18–19, 27,
    45–47, 59–60, 62–63, 65, 68, 82,
    88, 90, 96, 107, 111–121, 133,
    137, 140–142, 148, 153;
    Categories, 107; *Metaphysics,*
    108; *On Interpretation,* 107;
    Organon, 15, 107, 137; *Physics,*
    15, 107, 137; *Politics,* 115, 140;
    Posterior Analytics, 62, 107–109,
    118–119, 129, 144; *Prior*
    Analytics, 62, 107, 119, 144;
    Rhetoric, 1, 3, 5, 19, 31–32,
    45–47, 59, 65, 67, 69, 107, 111,
    115, 119–124, 126–129, 131,
    136–137, 140, 144–147, 153–154;
    Topics, 15–16, 107, 111, 118;
    Sophistical Refutations, 107
Arnhart, Larry, 2, 14, 17, 19,
    122–124, 137
Arrangement (*dispositio*), 24, 153
Ars dictaminis, 31, 34, 49
Ars poetriae, 31, 34, 92

Ars praedicandi, 4–5, 31, 33–34,
    49
Audience, 63–66, 73–76, 103,
    124–125, 127–128, 146–148
Augustine, 23, 31, 34

Bacchylides, 88
Bacon, Francis, 7
Bailey, Dudley, 56
Barr, James, 85
Barzizza, Gasperino, 35
Bede, 33
Benjamin, Walter, 90
Berlin, James, 71
Bitzer, Lloyd, 9, 18, 62, 65, 84
Black, Edwin, 9
Blair, Hugh, 50–51
Boethius, 33–34; *De topicis*
    differentiis, 33, 49
Bok, Derek C., 95
Bok, Sissela, 142, 151–152
Bowra, C. M., 88–89
Bramer, George R., viii, 3, 19–21,
    127, 135–155
Brannon, Lil, 2, 3
Brigham Young University, 96
Britton, James, 96
Bruner, Jerome, 12, 45
Bruni, Leonardo, 25, 39
Bulman, Raymond F., 90
Bultmann, Rudolf Karl, 84
Burke, Kenneth, 52–53, 55, 84, 96,
    104, 141. *See also* Pentad
Byron, William J., viii

Campbell, George, 8
Carnegie-Mellon University, 72
Cato, 30
Causality, 11, 18–19, 109–133. *See*
    also Cause(s)
Cause(s): Aristotle's four:

Gadamer, Hans-Georg, 84, 95
Gage, John, 2, 20, 65, 73, 77
Galilei, Galileo, 7
Galluzzi, Paolo, 7
Garin, Eugenio, 6
Gates, Rosemary, viii
Gerl, Hanna Barbara, 39
Gerson, Jean, 24
Gilleland, Donald, 99
Gleick, James, 57
Golden, James L., 28
Gorgias, 2, 23, 82, 89, 91–92, 151
Grammar, 5, 31, 37–38, 49, 104
Grassi, Ernesto, 38–40
Green, Lawrence, 73, 76
Grimaldi, William M. A., 15, 46,
  61–63, 65–67
Guarino da Verona, 34, 36

Hairston, Maxine C., viii, 10,
  15–17, 59–77, 125–127
Happiness, 68
Harmony, as ultimate aim of
  rhetoric, 139, 140, 142–143,
  148–150, 152
Harrington, David V., 20, 52
Harrington, Elbert W., 47
Hauser, Gerard A., 19
Hawes, Stephen, 27
Hayes, John, 72
Hegel, Georg W. F., 90
Heidegger, Martin, 84
Hermagoras, 28
Hermeneutics, 84, 104
Hesiod, 80, 87
Heurisis, 27
Hirsch, E. D., 84, 104
Hofstadter, Douglas R., 57
Homer, 80
Hope, Richard, 112
Horace, 34
Howell, Wilbur Samuel, 5
Humanism, civic, 5, 36
Humanities, 5, 7, 25–26, 32, 34,
  35–36, 38–40, 101, 105
Hume, David, 109–111, 114, 133

Imbemba, Kathleen Millar, viii
Induction, 10, 129–130
Intellect: practical, 65–67;
  speculative, 65–67
Invention, 9–10, 24, 29, 34, 36,
  43–57, 65, 75; first recorded
  mention of, 27
Isocrates, 23, 29, 87

Jesuits, 6, 19
Justice, 3, 87

Kairos, 1, 4, 17, 79–105; and
  aesthetics, 91–92; and
  education, 92–93; and
  epistemology, 88–90; and
  ethics, 87–88; and rhetoric, 91;
  definition, 80, 85–86. *See also*
  Appropriateness; Timeliness
Kant, Immanuel, 90
Keith, Philip M., 52
Kennedy, George, 2, 4, 7–8,
  31–33, 35, 137
Kerek, Andrew, 96
Kessler, Eckhard, 39
Kinneavy, James C., viii, 17–18,
  60, 69, 79–105, 138
Klaus, Carl H., 11
Kneupper, Charles, 52
Knoblauch, C. H., 2
Koestler, Arthur, 68
Kristeller, Paul Oskar, 6
Kuhn, Thomas S., 111

Lanham, Richard, 79
Laudan, Larry, 111
Lawyers, 12, 23
Lechner, Sr. Joan Marie, 50
Leff, Michael C., 47
Letter writing (*ars dictaminis*), 31,
  34, 49
Levi, Doro, 80–81, 83, 85, 88, 91,
  103
Liberal arts. *See* Humanities
Locke, John, 50, 110
Logic, 11, 62–63, 76–77, 104

scientific, 108–109, 117–119,
125–127, 144
Quintilian, 3, 12, 30–31, 33, 35,
47–48; *Institutio oratoria,* 30

Ramsey, Allen, 20, 151
Ramus, Peter, 6, 29, 38; Ramists,
8
Ratio studiorum, 6
Rhetoric: Ciceronian, 17, 80;
definition of, 25–26, 46, 100;
deliberative, 25, 122–123, 126;
as a discipline, 102, 104, 154;
epideictic, 25, 122–124,
126–127; Greek, 28, 89; judicial,
25, 28, 124–125, 126–127;
medieval, 4–5, 16, 23–24, 29–31,
34; Platonic, 17, 80, 89, 91;
neoclassical, 8; Platonic-
Aristotelian, 2, 3, 21;
Renaissance, 6, 19, 23–26,
29–30, 34, 48, 50; right,
135–155; Roman, 47–48, 50;
Sophistic, 17, 80
Rhetorical situation, 18, 73–74, 83
Richards, I. A., 138, 141
Roberts, W. Rhys, 47
Rogers, Carl, 141; Rogerian
argument, 76, 143, 155
Rohman, D. Gordon, 52–54, 71
Romanticism and composition,
70–72, 90
Ross, William D., 67
Rostagni, Augusto, 81–82, 85,
87–88, 91–92
Royal Society, 8
Russell, D. A. F. M., 28

Sages of Greece, Seven, 80–81
Schleiermacher, Friedrich, 95
Schoeck, Richard J., viii, 3–4,
12–13, 23–41
Science: Aristotelian, 15, 62, 108,
119, 144; modern, 7, 13, 39–40,
65, 68, 98, 101, 110, 120, 154;
philosophy of, 110–111

Seigel, Jerrold, 6
Semiotics, 41
Sentence-combining, 96
Sign *(semeion),* 120
Socrates, 86, 137, 139, 141–143,
151, 155
Solon, 80
Sophists, 1, 3, 17, 80–81, 83, 96,
138
Species, 14, 113
Speech communication, 104
Status, 3, 28, 108–109; and
Aristotle's scientific questions,
125–127, 144–145
Steiner, George, 39–40
Stock, Brian, 32
Stout, Barbara, viii
Structuralism, 104
Sturm, Johann, 30
Style, 153–154
Syllogism, 47, 50, 60–61, 69, 72,
131

Tagmemics, 13, 52, 84, 104
Telos, 1, 4, 114; as good, 115; as
terminal, 115. *See also* Aim(s);
End(s); Cause: final
Texas, University of, 96
Theognis, 87
Theology, 32–34, 84
Thierry of Chartres, 32
Thompson, Craig R., 35
Tillich, Paul, 17, 83, 85, 89–90, 96,
99
Timeliness *(kairos),* 80–81, 85,
88–90
Topics: common, 13, 45–47;
special, 13–14, 45–46
Topoi, 1, 4, 6, 11, 13–16, 26, 39,
43–57, 120, 128–129, 153. *See
also* Topics
Toulmin, Stephen, 11, 76–77
Trebizond, George of, 34–35
Tripp, Janice A., 52
Truth, 68, 136, 137–138, 142, 148.
See also Veracity